John Blickerdyke

Wild Sports in Ireland

John Blickerdyke

Wild Sports in Ireland

ISBN/EAN: 9783742899248

Manufactured in Europe, USA, Canada, Australia, Japa

Cover: Foto ©ninafisch / pixelio.de

Manufactured and distributed by brebook publishing software (www.brebook.com)

John Blickerdyke

Wild Sports in Ireland

WILD SPORTS IN IRELAND.

BY

JOHN BICKERDYKE.

Author of "Lady Val's Elopement," "A Banished Beauty," "Days in Thule," "Days of my Life," "The Book of the All-Round Angler," &c.

WITH ILLUSTRATIONS.

LONDON:
L. UPCOTT GILL, 170, STRAND, W.C.
1897.

CONTENTS.

CHAP.		PAGE
I.—A VOYAGE OF DISCOVERY		1
II.—MOONLIGHTERS		19
III.—IN CLONOOLIA BAY		41
IV.—AMONG THE CLARE HILLS		53
V.—BRIAN BORU'S SNIPE		81
VI.—A GILLAROO DAY		97
VII.—THE FISH THAT DID NOT FAIL		109
VIII.—WINTER SPORTS OF THE LAKE DWELLERS		119
IX.—SLOB TROUT		133
X.—ICEBOUND, AND A WILD-GOOSE CHASE		155
XI.—COMMENCING WITH YACHT RACING AND ENDING WITH A BAG OF PERCH		171
XII.—RUDD *versus* MEDICINE MAN		187
XIII.—THE FORTY POUND PIKE		195
XIV.—"TEMPEST TOSS'D"		209

ILLUSTRATIONS.

"MARRIED IN CAMERA" ... ... (FRONTISPIECE).	
	PAGE
"ONE OF THE MOST BEAUTIFUL ANCIENT CROSSES IN IRELAND"	9
ROUND TOWER AT CLONMACNOISE	11
"OH, BEGOR! AND IS IT THE BATTERING-RAM YOU HAVE BROUGHT AGAINST ME?"	21
"THEY THOUGHT I HAD COME TO SERVE A WRIT UPON THEM"	23
"I SAILED TO KILLALOE"	48
IRISH CHAR, PHOTOGRAPHED FROM LIFE	57
"A SLEEK DONKEY, BEARING PANNIERS LADEN WITH PEAT"	61
"ONE OF THE FEW IRISHMEN LEFT IN THE DISTRICT WHO STILL WORE KNEE-BREECHES"	64
LOUGH CREINA AND THE O'CALLAGHAN'S CABIN ...	73
"FROM BRIAN BORU'S CASTLE TO THE VILLAGE" ...	85

	PAGE
"THEY ARE MOSTLY SQUARE TOWERS"	89
"A BRIDGE OF FIVE LOW ARCHES"	137
"TINY STREAMLETS WERE GOOD SIZED RIVERS"	141
"A CHARMING PASTORAL SCENE"	145
THE SLOB-TROUT RIVERS	151
"THE POOR SHELTER OF A SHEBEEN" ...	198
"TAKEN FROM LIFE"	199
"ON THE HIGHER MOORLANDS"	215

PREFACE.

THERE is a class of readers whose love of sport and nature is immense, but whose lines are laid for the most part in uninteresting wildernesses of bricks and mortar. Letters often reach me from such sources, and I gather that books of sporting reminiscences appeal most strongly, and bring feelings of delight, tempered maybe with regret, if they contain a whiff of the heather and turf reek, wafted through sunlight by breezes, perhaps brine-laden, to the music of rippling, gurgling streams, roaring rivers, or lake wavelets breaking on the shore. *Days in Thule with Rod, Gun, and Camera*, and *Days of My Life on Waters Fresh and Salt*, made me many friends among the class I refer to, and I venture to hope that this latest effort of my pen will not be less pleasing to them and other readers than the two books of like character, which have gone before.

The present volume consists for the most part of pages from out the history of my life spent on wild inland seas, or on the borders of the Shannon estuary. I have also given sundry items of information likely to be of use to sportsmen visiting Ireland. No methodic arrangement of chapters has been followed, except the method of being unmethodic for the sake of obtaining frequent change of scene and subject. I am responsible for most of the whole-page illustrations which will, I hope, lend interest to the book; but have to acknowledge with thanks the views of Clonmacnoise and Killaloe, reproduced on pages 7, 9, 48, and 85, lent me by Mr. Lawrence, of Dublin, the well-known photographer of picturesque Ireland. I must further gratefully acknowledge my indebtedness to the Editors of the *Graphic*, *Field*, and *Fishing Gazette*, for having enabled me to reprint certain portions of the book which were serialised in their columns, but have since been to a large extent re-written.

Herein is so much concerning moonlighters, battering-rams, and the like, that some doubts may, perhaps, be raised in the minds of nervous persons as to whether Ireland is really a safe country for the stranger who goes there on sport intent. Let me therefore say here that statistics prove beyond question how for years there has been considerably more crime per head of the population in England than in Ireland. As a matter of fact, it is a far more dangerous proceeding to promenade the Thames Embankment in London, after midnight, than to spend a night in a tent among the mountains of Connemara or Galway.

At the present time there is a singular lull in the Irish agrarian agitation, and no place in Europe is more quiet and safe than the Sister Isle. Even during the worst times, when the feeling against England and the English was very strong on account of the repressive measures which were adopted to pacify the country, with the exception of a little incident in connection with a discharged servant, to be hereafter related, I never had rough word or black look from any man, rich or poor, in Ireland. The only way in which a dispute between the English sportsman and the Irish peasantry would be likely to arise, would be in connection with a raid by peasants who claimed sporting rights over some piece of the mountain on which the shooting had been let. But even such incidents can be counted on the fingers of one hand, and at the present time are most improbable.

It is not for me to enter into an exhaustive consideration of Irish troubles, but I venture to say poverty is at the root of most of them, and that the more sportsmen visit its mountains, bogs, rivers and loughs, leaving English gold behind them in exchange for Irish salmon, white trout, gillaroo, grouse, and snipe, the better it will be for the "distressed counthry." But though the accommodation is in places all that the most fastidious can desire, before Ireland becomes, like Scotland, a popular resort for sportsmen, the hotel arrangements generally must be vastly improved, and owners of property might well devote a little trouble and expense to the better preservation of their moors and rivers. Even now, Ireland is a paradise for the sportsman of small means who does not mind roughing it; houses with extensive fishing and shooting rights may be had for absurdly low rents, and household expenses are small. Apart from life in private houses, hotels, and lodgings, the country offers great possibilities of enjoyment to those who love a free, wild, open-air existence—men who are never happier than when under canvas or cruising on strange waters in a well found yacht or canoe—and canoes must be staunch and sea-worthy for this purpose. Take it on the whole I am inclined to think there can be no more delightful way of spending a few months than, as I did, to become a modern lake-dweller on the Shannon and its stormy, mountain-surrounded loughs. One thing the Briton who crosses the Irish Channel for the first time will be well advised to do—let him leave his British pride and hauteur at home. Irishmen as a rule absolutely decline to be driven, but are easily led by anyone possessing a kindly, genial manner, with just a touch of enthusiasm concerning the matter in hand, whatever it may be.

I cannot close this chat preliminary without bearing testimony to the great kindness and hospitality shown me by many Irish families, and, in fact, by people of all classes with whom I came in contact during my wanderings. It gives me the greatest possible pleasure to dedicate this volume of Irish Sporting Sketches to my friends at Paradise, Youghal, Meelick, Mountshannon, Raheens, and Killaloe.

JOHN BICKERDYKE.

Elmlea, South Stoke, Oxon.
February, 1897.

A Voyage of Discovery.

"*Solomon in his parables saith that a good spirit maketh a flowering age, that is, a fair age and a long. And sith it is so, I ask this question, Which be the means and the causes that induce a man into a merry spirit? Truly, to my best discretion, it seemeth good disports and honest games in whom a man joyeth without any repentance after. Then followeth it that good disports and honest games be cause of man's fair age and long life.*"

"The Book of St. Albans," A.D. 1486.

"*O mistress mine, where are you roaming?
O stay and hear; your true love's coming,
 That can sing both high and low.
Trip no further, pretty sweeting,
Journeys end in lovers meeting
 Every wise man's son doth know.*"

SHAKESPEARE.

Wild Sports in Ireland.

CHAPTER I.

A VOYAGE OF DISCOVERY.

My first visit to the non-tidal waters of the noble Shannon was brought about in a somewhat curious manner. There appeared one Saturday in an English sporting paper a letter which must have set the heart of every pike fisher who read it throbbing. The writer was an informing Irish maker or vendor of fishing tackle. He stated that in his district pike were caught up to 40lb. and 50lb., and thirty-pounders were quite common.

I had been long stricken with the big-pike fever, and here obviously was the place for the English angler, weary of wasting his strength in spinning for little fellows of 10lb. and 15lb. A letter was dispatched to Ireland to inquire of this good-natured tackle maker the names of the lakes, the accommodation to be had, and so forth. In the course of a fortnight a reply came from the man's widow. She said her husband had died since writing the letter (which was not surprising), and she had no knowledge of the lakes to which he referred. There was a postscript; she still carried on the business, would be happy to supply the tackle, and so forth. Thus it fell out that the secret of the lakes where pike were caught up to 40lb. and 50lb., thirty-pounders being common, was lost to the world. Those prolific waters have yet to be discovered.

At this time I was an innocent young undergraduate, and taking into my confidence a friend, who was almost as fond of fishing as myself, the determination was arrived at to make a most vigorous onslaught on these Irish pike during the Christmas vacation. But where to go was the great difficulty. Every Irish lake seemed to have yielded pike of from 40lb. to 100lb. at some time or other, but in each case there was wanting that amount of corroborative evidence which would justify us in making a considerable journey.

A trifle disheartened by the death of the tackle-maker, but nothing daunted, we next sent a letter to the paper inquiring of the world at large where the big Irish pike of which we had so often heard could be caught. There were several replies. One writer strongly recommended us to visit Lough Rea, a big Shannon lough, which he declared abounded in enormous fish, and was in addition swarming with wildfowl during the winter months. We were both almost as keen on wild duck as pike, and the description appealed to us strongly. Researches into red-covered books and atlases disclosed the fact that the nearest town of any importance to this fishing ground was Athlone, and thither my friend D., his two brothers, who were to spend a fortnight with us, and myself journeyed, arriving at The Royal one cold January afternoon. On the way over, one sentimental member of the party confided to the rest that there dwelt near Athlone a young lady between whom and himself certain tender passages had passed in years gone by; and that it would give him the greatest delight to have some news of her. Thus entered a spice of romance into the expedition.

The first question on arriving at the hotel was the usual one asked by every angler: "Any fishing been done lately?" The landlord thought it was too early for the salmon, but he would ask Mick about it. Or was it pike we were after? There were a great many pike in the lake, but no one fished for them at that time of the year; he would send for Mick after dinner anyway.

And after dinner little red-haired Mick Flannigan, water bailiff and fisherman, made his appearance, was offered and accepted a glass, and forthwith proceeded to throw cold water over our young hopes: There was not a man in the place, said he, who would dream of fishing for pike at that time of the year. Pike were only caught there in the summer. It was true the lake was full of them, bad cess to them, but divil a one would we catch, however much we tried.

When four Englishmen travel several hundred miles,

and cross the Irish Channel in winter, for the purpose of catching fish, they are not the sort of people to go home without making a trial of the water. Mick's ideas were secretly laughed at, and before going to bed we agreed between ourselves that the truth was, the Irish did not know anything about catching pike and were afraid of the cold. Why, was not sport at its very best during the winter, as every pike fisher well knew? If we could get some other man than Mr. Flannigan it might be as well.

But on the morrow, as there was no one else whom the landlord would recommend, Mick and his boat were engaged for a week. Armed with rods, spoonbaits, phantoms, clippers, and other artificials, we set forth up the Shannon, and so on into the lake, and trolled all day long, sometimes deep, sometimes shallow, sometimes by dead reed beds, sometimes by rocky shores, but never getting so much as a pull from a pike. When evening came Mick looked at us as much as to say, "I tould ye so!"

The next day guns were taken out in the boat, some wildfowl were shot, and further attempts were made to catch a pike, but without success. Among the birds shot was a coot, and, to the astonishment of everyone at the inn, including Mick, this was ordered to be skinned and cooked for dinner. While it was roasting there entered the kitchen one of those vagrants who wander from house to house in Ireland and live on the gifts of the good-natured peasantry. Seeing the bird, he asked what it was, and being told crossed himself, and muttering that it was a "strange thing indade to eat, for sure wasn't it the bird that betrayed our Saviour?"

Mick, who had come in after dinner to receive orders for the following day, told the story, and added that a certain "Meejor Brown," for whom he had worked, used to eat coots boiled, "and very good they wor, too," said Mick. Now, a boiled coot, unless it be skinned and treated in a certain manner by which its strength of flavour may be diminished, is a most un-toothsome morsel, much resembling the flavour of a doubtful oyster. We four, though young, knew this, and believing that Mick, who declared the skinning to be unnecessary, was laughing at us in his sleeve, determined to be even with him.

The following day occurred the great event of the week. Three of us gave up fishing and went by ourselves in a boat up the lake shooting, while I, retaining the services of Mick, stuck to the section of the river between the town and the lake, and trolled and trolled and spun and spun, casting out in Thames fashion, all through the short winter's day. Just as Mick was denouncing this foolish plan of casting out a bait like that (as if any dacent pike would take it!) there came a very slight pull at the rod-point, and behold! I had hooked, and ultimately brought into the boat, a pike which weighed just one and a quarter pounds!

It was not a big fish certainly, hardly a bait for a forty-pounder, but it enabled us to point out to Mick how very wrong he was in declaring it impossible to catch pike in that part of the world in winter.

Finding the river so fruitful of sport, we decided to journey next day down stream to the old ruins of the Seven Churches, at Clonmacnoise, trailing spoon baits there and back, and taking the guns on the chance of getting within range of mallard, plover, or wily curlew. A hamper of provisions was part of the cargo, and one of us gave certain special directions regarding the lunch provided for Mick Flannigan. Not a shot was fired nor a pike hooked on the way down to the old ruins. But Mick enlivened the journey by the story of certain English soldiers who, when garrisoned at Athlone for the first time, went down the river shooting, being told there were abundance of wildfowl, and returned with fifteen tame ducks which they had shot in all innocence.

In due course we arrived at Clonmacnoise and inspected round tower, ruins of the Seven Churches, and the holy well. In the graveyard is one of the most beautiful ancient crosses in Ireland, of which I am glad to give an illustration. On page 11 may be seen the round tower of Clonmacnoise, with its door many feet from the ground. This indicates that at times these problematic structures were besieged, and that their occupants found it desirable to enter by a ladder which they would doubtless draw up after them. I shall have a word to say concerning these towers in a subsequent chapter.

There is a legend that at night the peasants hear

silvery-toned church bells tolling beneath the great
river. Some robbers, so the story runs, pilfered the

Ancient Irish Cross at Clonmacnoise.

belfry, and appropriately ended their wicked lives by the
foundering of their boat while crossing the river. The

bells sank, but are rung by other than mortal hands on occasions. Sight-seeing over, the hamper of provisions was unpacked. Then followed the joke of the day, Mick being handed half a loaf and a whole, boiled, unskinned coot. Being a respectful man, he retired to eat his lunch, but his hiding-place was noted, and when the time came for him to bail out the boat, which leaked after the manner of all true Irish craft, a search was made, and there, hidden away among rank grass, lay the whole of the bird, cooked as recommended by "Meejor Brown," but neglected, uncared for, untouched. As to the excellence of boiled coot nothing further was heard from Mick, who maintained a grave silence during the homeward journey.

In the evening the romantic member of our party, who, it seemed, had hitherto forgotten his little romance in the interests of his new surroundings and the hunt after phantom pike—suddenly remembered sweet Kathleen Malone—so let her be called—and questioned the waiter about her. The Malones were a big family, said the waiter; Miss Kathleen was it? Sure, wasn't that the one with the hooked nose? The romantic one reluctantly admitted that the young lady had rather a prominent nose; but his face lengthened considerably when Mick declared:

"She married the dochter, has five childers, and has grown very fat intoirely."

Certainly there are other disillusions in life than those concerning Irish pike.

Among the replies we received to our newspaper letter of inquiry respecting big Irish pike was one from a gentleman residing on the banks of Lough Derg, who had a yacht to let.

ROUND TOWER AT CLONMACNOISE.

Before our week was up at Athlone we came to the conclusion that we had made a grand mistake in attacking the

Lough Rea pike in winter, and hearing that there was wild-fowl shooting to be obtained on Derg resolved to hire the yacht if it was still available. As to this there was no difficulty.

The old craft was sent up the river to meet us at Meelick. She was a fine, roomy, round-bottomed, cranky old vessel, formerly possessing a huge centre-board, the removal of which, to make the cabin more convenient, had by no means increased her stability. But she was well-sailed by our skipper, a man who knew every inch of the lake, and was invariably called Sinbad. His parents never intended him to be thus known, but it so happened that in his master's service were two James Gliesons—he being one of them—the other tending to stable work. To distinguish between the pair, our skipper was called "the sailor," which was very soon changed to "Sinbad." Our crew consisted of a fine young fellow called Jim Hall, who had served a long apprenticeship to the rocks, waves, and wind-storms of the Shannon, in one of the black-hulled turf boats which trade between the peat bogs and the towns where fuel is scarce.

We arrived at Meelick, and went on board just as evening was closing in, and wild-fowl of various kinds were so much in evidence that I determined to rise early the next morning and shoot a few.

Given an average amount of practice and a reasonably straight eye, shooting is very much a matter of health and nerve. I had been in Ireland just long enough to derive considerable benefit from the change of air and out-door life, combined with plenty of hard exercise ; for we all took our share at rowing the boat when hunting those disappointing pike. I venture to suppose, from what happened to me that day, I had about attained to the peculiar degree of fitness which is generally attributed to fiddles. It was practically dark when we commenced shooting, but now and again an object would rise out of the reeds through which I was being punted, and instantly wing away into the darkness unless I fired, when it would surely fall headlong into the water.

Every shot seemed a hopeless one, but, strange to say, I did not pull trigger that morning without bringing down my bird, though to our disgust, coots, which were indistinguishable in the twilight of early morning, formed a very large proportion of my bag. I never shot so well before or since, and, making no pretensions of being anything more than an average shot, experienced exceeding astonishment at the way the birds tumbled down whenever I put my gun to my shoulder. And the worst of it was that I went up ever so many pegs in the esteem of our skipper, only to fall again most lamentably some days later, when, after dining out at a hospitable friend's, much of that fiddle-like fitness temporarily disappeared.

About eight o'clock, when we had breakfast, I brought back a considerable number of birds to the yacht, and an hour later, with a fair wind right aft, we set all sail and hied away down the broad river.

Tall reeds fringed the banks on every side, and it was

a happy thought to steer the yacht close to the right-hand shore and let the boom out over the starboard side, sweeping the reeds, and putting up any duck that were in them. As the birds rose D. or I shot them. My good luck continued, for never a bird failed to get his quietus, or even required the second barrel; in fact, the number of times the yacht had to run into the wind and lie to, to enable us to pick up the birds, somewhat tried the patience of our amiable and willing crew.

Before nightfall we were on the bosom of great Derg, the grandest and stormiest of all the Shannon loughs, and spent a glorious time there, though at that season of the year the pike were no more amenable to our artificial baits than those of Lough Rea. In four weeks we caught one pikelet between us, that is, so far as the lake was concerned; but in several tributary streams we took a fair number of fish, running from two to six or seven pounds. Our best, and indeed only good fishing, we owed to some relatives of the owner of the yacht, who, sympathising much with our disappointment in the matter of pike, very kindly invited us to fish a little private lake of their own.

The place was situated in what may be termed the wilds of Tipperary, far from any railway, and with no other house near for miles, except the miserable cabins of the peasants. Our good friends had tried an interesting experiment on this lake, having made it a rule for many years to allow no gun to be fired on it, or within any considerable distance of it. The natural result was that wild-fowl of many kinds congregated there, and the whole place was alive with mallards, teal, widgeon, mergansers, sheldrake, and other beautiful birds.

The little sheet of water swarmed with rudd and pike, and we were recommended, if we wished to get a really big fish, to bring some small trout with us, and use them on live-bait tackle. Previous experience had led me to disbelieve somewhat in the efficacy of trout, and there was also a feeling, which will be shared by many a fly fisher, that to destroy a trout for the sake of catching a pike is an offence against the canons of sport. So I stuck to a venerable red phantom which had proved successful in some Irish waters during the winter months.

It was a beautiful spot. The lawn sloped from the house down to the edge of the lake, and along the banks grew graceful ash and poplar trees which overhung the still, dark water. In the centre of the lake was a bed of dead brown weeds, among which were wild-fowl innumerable. These quacked and splashed and gambolled in the most unconcerned way, knowing full well that none venturing there would harm them. For half-an-hour an attempt at live-baiting with a trout was made, but no single run was obtained. Then the rod was laid on the bank, the float tackle with the trout attached was left in the water, trimmer fashion, and we all rowed off, spinning round the big central reed bed. Strange to say, not a single pike would run at a troutling which, on very suitable tackle, one of us spun over their noses, but the old, half-worn-out phantom, killed fish after fish ; and when our hospitable host insisted on our leaving the boat and going up to the house for lunch, there was quite a fine show of pike varying from 4lb. to 10lb. laid out on the steps of the hall door.

The enthusiastic and persevering angler often has a good deal to say concerning the lunch or dinner offered him by kind friends who are unused to the ways of fish and sportsmen. If it be a dinner, it invariably comes just at the time when, after a long, fruitless day, the angler perceives that the trout are commencing to rise. If it be lunch in winter, it will as surely interfere with his being on the water at the very time the fish are commencing to feed. Many a man prefers indépendence at an inn to the most luxurious quarters with friends on this account, for it is not everyone who will appreciate the necessity of upsetting the regular meal times so that a few more fish may be caught. Who is there can say to his host, "My dear sir, you are very kind to invite me to dinner, but I hold the rise of fish of greater importance than your invitation, and so must decline it"? Perhaps there may be a few such men, but certainly not many.

This occasion was like many more. Fish had been feeding for about an hour before we went in to lunch, so that we probably missed the best hour and a-half of the day, and in the afternoon, when we re-entered the boat, had considerable difficulty in adding to our basket. Perhaps the strangest thing about the day's fishing was that the live trout on the float tackle, which had been working about in one of the most pikey corners of the whole water—a place which we had hardly rowed over once without getting a run—was untouched. The pike would have nothing to say to it. In such a spot as this, where birds, old and young, were so numerous, a pike fly ought to have worked great execution, but with this bait we were not provided. Certainly, nothing could have been better than the red phantom, a bait which usually kills exceedingly well wherever pike are to be caught in Ireland during the winter. In summer it is not nearly so deadly, pike then appearing to prefer a blue, brown, or silvery bait.

It was not until some years after our "voyage of discovery" that I succeeded in catching a pike over 20lb., though I gave the forty-pounders many opportunities of being caught.

I had taken over with me to Ireland that year a large-mouthed glass bottle containing spirits of wine, in which was pickled a few dozens of Thames bleak and gudgeon. They had been some years in the spirit and were shrivelled, but the bleak, which had turned yellow and had lost all their silveryness, proved a far more deadly bait for pike and trout than the most gorgeous of artistic artificials. I used to spin them on a Chapman spinner, for by no possibility could they have been put on any other form of spinning tackle. It was with one of these mummified Thames bleak that I caught my largest Irish pike.

Jim Brady, the boy I impressed in my service after the little boycott described in the following chapter, was rowing me. The time was about the middle of October, the pike were at their primest, and we were slowly working along the edge of the big shallow which is dominated by the ancient castle near the mouth of Scariff Bay. Suddenly there was a good substantial pull at the end of the rod, and I roundly abused Jim for taking me into all too shoal water, for there was certainly not more than eight feet under us, which is a small depth for pike fishing in a big lake like Lough Derg. The rock on which I had caught soon began to move, not in a very lively fashion, perhaps, but in a steady, resolute way, to which I dared offer little resistance, for my tackle was fine.

I wish I could record a series of brilliant dashes and leaps and rushes on the part of the fish, but so long as I adhere to the truth, I can do nothing of the kind; and have a strong suspicion that those remarkable contests with pike which we read about in the newspapers are written by gentlemen who are of a romantic temperament. It is a comparatively rare thing for a pike to make a long and determined dash for liberty. The nearest approach to anything of the kind occurred to me when I had hooked one of the biggest pike of my life. It was in the Thames, near Bolney islands. The fellow, after playing sullenly for a few minutes, allowed himself to be brought to the boat's side, but the sight of the landing-net gave him such a shock to his nerves that he scuttled off almost along the top of the water

A VOYAGE OF DISCOVERY.

in the direction of the shore, and literally leaped into the reeds which fringed the bank, just as a dog would plunge into them after a coot or water rat. He rose quite two feet in the air, and came down with a splash. The line appeared to hold, but on my getting the boat up to the spot I simply found a triangle fixed in a reed, and the fish nowhere to be seen. That was a much more exciting contest than the one I had with the twenty-five pound pike.

Strong was this Irish fish, you may believe me, but certainly within fifteen minutes I had him up to the side of the boat, when Jim gaffed him near the tail. I am ashamed to say that the handle of the gaff was old and unreliable, and fearing a break I got Jim to hold the gaff while I put my fingers in the eyes of the fish, and we brought him in together—I should say "her," because it turned out to be a female. There she lay at the bottom of the boat, as beautiful a picture of a pike as an angler could wish to gaze upon—small in the head, thick in the shoulder, and without that great potbelly which is the defect in most large pike. I was very anxious not to injure her appearance in killing her, and the killing was a matter of no small difficulty, for she showed certain vicious propensities, and failing to catch hold of any of our legs, grasped one of the timbers of the boat and scrunched it up between her teeth.

The end soon came, and she now rests in a glass case over my dining-room mantelpiece; and I hope the epitaph which Mr. Williams, the clever Dublin taxidermist,

B

has placed in the corner of the case is more truthful than such inscriptions usually are, for he states her weight to be twenty-five pounds, and I had no means of weighing her myself, though I made a feeble attempt in that direction with the spring out of a steam launch pressure guage.

To give an idea of the frequency with which monster pike are caught in such lakes as Lough Derg, where they are popularly supposed to abound, I may add that I could get to hear of no pike so large as mine having been taken out of the lough for several years.

I must not end this paper without a word of praise for the sailors of the Shannon. They are, as a rule, capital fellows, and keener hands in a race I have never seen. In winter they have to turn their hand to anything, and their accomplishments are most varied. I know one who is not only a good sailor, rigger, and sailmaker, but also an excellent carpenter, plumber, painter, gamekeeper, groom, and fisherman, and plays the flute and pipes.

Moonlighters.

"*The rising moon has hid the stars;*
Her level rays, like golden bars,
  Lie on the landscape green,
   With shadows brown between.
And silver-white the river gleams,
As if Diana in her dreams,
   Had dropt her silver bow
   Upon the meadows low."

LONGFELLOW.

"*Speak! Speak! thou fearful guest!*
Who, with thy hollow breast
Still in rude armour drest,
   Camest to daunt me;
Wrapt not in Eastern balms,
But with thy fleshless palms
Stretched as if asking alms,
   Why dost thou haunt me?"

IBID.

CHAPTER II.

MOONLIGHTERS.

But, if the pike of the Shannon would not feed in winter, they were fairly complacent one autumn, when, after being all but wrecked in a bay which was accounted a safe mooring ground, I took the yacht up the mouth of a certain river for shelter. Therefrom we trolled a rent-fringed portion of the lake, which was very prolific in fish.

Undergraduate days were over, and with my wife I had been spending, on yachtboard, a most enjoyable summer, which, generally speaking, was unmarred by the conflict then proceeding between the Irish landlords and the peasantry. In fact, the incidents I am about to relate happened during one of the darkest years of Ireland's history. Of the political aspects of the case, of the rights and wrongs of landlord and tenant, I say nothing. My task is simply to tell of things just as they fell out, only changing the names of the river and locality for reasons which may be obvious.

On all sides was striking evidence of the serious state of affairs in the Sister Isle. Some families lived in almost a state of siege. Here and there miniature fortresses were erected, loopholed for rifles, and garrisoned by members of the R.I.C. Dinners and other social gatherings were foregone, for who would drive out at night when murder lurked behind stone walls? In the south or west few landlords' lives were safe. At one house I visited even the ladies had taken to revolver practice, and great iron shutters, supposed to be bulletproof, covered the windows of the room in which we dined. At another place, ten miles distant, the colonel was driving his beasts to market while his wife turned dairymaid, for all their people had fled.

Among the tenants evictions were common, the battering ram was a standing and effective institution, and the suffering and misery of the poorer classes was no whit less than that of their wealthier neighbours.

As an Englishman, visiting the country for sporting purposes, I deemed myself tolerably safe ; but there came a day when a drunken Irish servant had to be dismissed, and no other person, though some were willing, would take his place, for none dared.

There are many advantages in life on yachtboard. For instance, without notice to the enemy, one can sail many miles away in a few hours. There is no car ride along roads which may be infested by men with blackened faces, and carrying bludgeons or the more cowardly firearm. The journey may be made secretly and silently. Pat awakes in the morning, looks over the water, and sees that the Englishman and his floating castle have disappeared.

In a thinly populated country twenty miles is a great distance; we found at the end of it a "boy" who knew nothing of our little boycott at Mount Kilrush, and was only too glad to form one of the crew of the white-winged *Tern*. Thus was Pat Brady secured for three months.

"OH! BEGOR! AND IS IT THE BATTERING-RAM YOU HAVE BROUGHT AGAINST ME?"

With the exception of this little difficulty about a servant I never had the slightest unpleasantness with the Irish peasantry, although I was in the country at a period which was perhaps worse than any during the past half-century. The battering-ram was in common use, and when putting up my large whole-plate camera one day to obtain a picture of a tumble-down old cottage and potato garden which I had come across—a small oasis in many miles of moorland—an old man came towards me with pale face and trembling, and said nervously, "Oh! begor! and is it the battering-ram you have brought against me?" He had heard of battering-rams and photography, but never seen either the landlord's door-opener or a camera. The illustration on page 21 is the result of that photograph, and the old fellow himself may be seen standing among the ruins

When approaching another cottage with the intention of getting the people belonging to it to pose as figures in a photographic picture, the women rushed shrieking into the house and bolted the door. O'Brien, the coachman, who was with me, explained that they thought I had come to serve a writ upon them, as their rent was overdue some time, and it was with great difficulty I made them believe I was not a process-server, and persuaded one of the bare-legged girls to be part and parcel of my photograph. And there she is standing in the picture, but in an anything but graceful pose; indeed, she seemed so terrified that I feared if I said much more to her about a natural position, easy pose, and so forth, she would probably run away

* * * * *

After an absence of about a fortnight, we returned to our old moorings in the Kilrush river, for there were the largest pike and the greatest number of wildfowl.

The morning after our arrival Pat was sent on shore to get provisions. He was absent two hours, but on his return, no sooner had he set foot on deck, and the

"THEY THOUGHT I HAD COME TO SERVE A WRIT UPON THEM."

hamper of groceries and butcheries had been lifted over the side, than he said:

"I want to leave, yer honour."

"Why?"

"Sure the boys will kill me if I shtop."

I assured him that the boys should not hurt him, and that he should not be sent on shore, but availed nothing. Finally, I hardened my heart, for I did not believe in the dangers he imagined, and threatened him with loss of wages, which were not payable until the end of the quarter, and a summons for breach of his contract of hiring. Thereat he blubbered copiously, and finally consented to stay with me until the end of the three months. Had the timorous fellow been in any particular danger I would not have kept him, but I knew that those who had threatened him were only one or two drinking mates of the fellow I had dismissed, and that from them he could be protected without difficulty. Moreover, I had made many good friends among the people in Mount Kilrush. But, as I have said, times were bad in Ireland then, and the lad was frightened.

Fright is somewhat infectious. There were two guns, a rifle, and a revolver on board, and I began to wonder if a visit might not be paid us some fine night by Captain Moonlight for the purpose of obtaining firearms for his company. Owing to the terrible gales which blew that October, one of which, as I have said, almost wrecked us, we had been forced to moor a little way inside the mouth of the river, and were only a few yards from the bank. Some miles higher up the stream was one of the most lawless towns in Ireland. What was to prevent half a dozen of its inhabitants rowing down any night and boarding the yacht? Even should this happen, I did not think for a moment that harm would be done us, unless we showed fight; but those guns were certainly tempting. Besides I *might* have shown fight, and it would have needed a very superior force to make me give up my favourite chokebore without a struggle. So when I slept a loaded revolver lay ready to my hand.

We had been moored about three weeks in the river. Lying awake one night, wondering if I should ever catch one of the monster, perhaps fabulous, pike which had originally enticed me to the Shannon, I heard the report of a gun. Dressed, or, rather, undressed as I was, I hurried on deck, but the night was pitchy dark, and nothing could be seen.

"Did you hear it, Pat?" said I, calling down the fore hatch.

"Hear what, sur?"

"A shot."

"Sorra a shot have I heard, yer honour. It's asleep I was."

There was nothing to be done, though I felt sure the gun had been fired for no good purpose, as the night was far too dark for any wildfowler to be abroad.

The following morning Pat went to get some water for the kettle, and, on his way to the spring, called at a cabin for the milk. He brought back word of a dastardly outrage.

In a cottage not 200 yards away from our moorings dwelt an old man with his wife; the woman much younger than her husband. Their little farm consisted of the grass land for a cow, a patch of potatoes, and a few acres of oats. At harvest time labour is very scarce in Ireland, owing to so many of the able-bodied men having emigrated, and thus it came about that if this old man, whom I will call O'Brien, had not been able to hire a machine to cut and bind his oats, the crop ran the risk of seeding on to the ground and being more or less spoilt.

In the district were two reaping machines — one owned by Malone, a farmer, who had sinfully paid his rent when it was due, and so was duly boycotted; the other belonging to a combination of farmers, and known as "the Land League machine."

Like a true patriot, O'Brien sought the services of the Land League reaper, but was told that he could not have it for four weeks, as others also wanted it. This placed him in a quandary. In a month's time his oats would not be worth the cutting. He was too old to reap them himself, and there was no labour to be obtained. His patriotism was not proof in this extremity. He hired the boycotted Malone's machine and saved his oats, but incurred the enmity of certain of his neighbours, who, perhaps thinking that love of country should be stronger than love of oats, resolved to punish him.

O'Brien's cot was different from most of the cabins thereabouts, inasmuch as it was of two stories, and had a slated roof. A solitary tree grew close to and partly overhung it. The kitchen-living room was on the ground floor—a comfortable enough place in the evening after "the pigs had ceased from troubling, and the chickens were at roost"—among the rafters. On the dark night of the shot, a band of patriots came to O'Brien's cottage ; one climbed the tree, and fired down through the roof, doubtless aiming as well as he could at the old man's bed. I daresay the pierced slate is there to this day, it not being fashionable in Ireland to mend holes.

Illness is not usually good fortune, but a slight attack of rheumatism, or one of those other evils that people must look for who live on the borders of bogs and swamps, had caused O'Brien to sleep that night belowstairs in the room heated by glowing peat embers. The patriot in the tree consequently fired into an empty room, but, not knowing this, went home happy in the feeling that he had done his duty by his country. The next morning the constabulary appeared, looked at the hole in the slate, and left two of their number to guard the old man. In a day or two a little loop-holed fortress was put up close to the cottage, and for some months six policemen watched over O'Brien, looking on when he dug up his potatoes, and following him to market. I believe the ungrateful man grumbled at being haunted by the force in this manner ; but had it been otherwise, he might soon have been in a position to haunt the constabulary. The people who grumbled most, however, were the patriotic farmers in the neighbourhood, who had between them to pay the expenses of maintaining the fortress. Finding this costly, they made no further attempt to punish people in that district for placing oats before patriotism, at least, not with rifles.

It was not unpleasant to feel that a fortified hut full of policemen was almost within hail of the yacht, though I had reason to regret that two of O'Brien's brave defenders were enthusiastic anglers, for each morning they skimmed over some of the best fishing grounds long before I was out of my bunk. One day, however, I rose early, before any members of the Royal Irish had put their eyes to their loopholes, and was rewarded by bringing home eight pike varying from 4lbs. to 7lb. In the afternoon I did a little shooting, had a portion of one of the pike for dinner, followed by a wild duck, and in due course turned in.

The following morning, soon after daybreak, Pat woke us by hammering on the bulkhead. I rose and went in to him.

"Whist," said he, mysteriously, "arrah, don't let the misthress hear."

"Hear what?"

"It's the fish—they're stholen!"

One can bear the loss of a few pike with fortitude, not to say indifference. But the man's face was white, and he trembled, and if the pike had gone, some one must have taken them. If we were to be boarded in this fashion, where would it stop? The fish had been laid on the deck over night. They were stone dead. Every one had disappeared.

We held a council of war, but could make nothing of

it. A boat could hardly have come alongside in the night without making some noise, as the least sound is heard all over a small yacht. In country districts, too, the Irish rarely steal things, but those marauding moonlighters might do anything. Pat was very much upset, and besought me to ask the Royal Irish Constabulary to protect us.

"Go up to the police hut and tell them about it," said I. "They may like to come and look at the place where the pike lay last night."

But Pat seemed disinclined to leave the yacht just then, and after breakfast two members of that splendid body of men, the R.I.C., came wandering down the bank, so I told them of the incident. As I had suggested to my man, they made a point of looking at the place where the fish had lain on the deck, and then gave it as their official opinion that the pike were no longer there, and that somebody must have removed them. Pat was much upset about the matter, and carried his feelings so evidently in his face that more than once the officers turned a suspicious glance upon him. But my crew was honesty itself, and I would hear no word against them.

"You have a clue?" said I, interrogatively.

Not being English detectives, the members of the R.I.C. at once admitted that they had not.

The matter remained a mystery.

Two nights later another pike was quietly stolen from the deck without our hearing anything, and with shame I confess it, I began to harbour unworthy susspicious of the R.I.C.

When I next caught some fish Pat had orders to leave them on deck at night and to pass a line through their gills, bringing the end of it down into the cuddy where he slept. He did as I directed, and, further, tied a piece of wood at the end of the line, so that if the fish were moved the wood would hit something and wake him up.

About one o'clock the following morning he came to me and said that the piece of wood had moved, and that "some one was afther taking the pike." I seized my revolver, and rushed out of the cabin. There was sufficient moonlight to enable me to see all over the yacht's deck and from one side of the river to the other. There was no one in sight. I called Pat to come up and see for himself that no one was there.

"You dreamt it," said I.

Pat was examining the pike, which still lay on the deck, and suddenly burst forth excitedly: "Sorra a bit did I drame it. Look at that now. Sure some one is afther removing the fish. Didn't I place them by one another just as if they were brothers, and now they're all anyway? It must be the fairies as is plaguing us. Oh! wirra, wirra! why didn't your honour let a poor boy go home when he wanted to? This is a dreadful place entoirely."

I never knew what Pat's little simile about brothers lying all of a row meant, unless he had a hazy recollection of his childhood, when he and his brothers slept seven in a bed, as he once told me. Nor for some time was any light thrown on the robbery. For the sake of our nerves, as much as to save our fish, we left no more pike on the deck.

Some three days after the visit from the—fairies shall I say?—Pat came to me, smiling all over his face, and asked me to go ashore with him. He took me a little way along the bank, parted the sedge, and there, cushioned on the moss, were the heads and bones of the pike which had been stolen, or most of them. Each bone was as clean as a Dutch dairy.

"Didn't I say them robbers was the good people," said he, triumphantly.

"You did, Pat," said I. "But tell me, is *fairy* another name for *rat* in Ireland?"

"Begor! I suppose it must be that," said the boy, with a grin.

We both felt considerably relieved to find that our moonlight visitors were of such a harmless species. Evidently rats in great force must have visited the yacht, dragged the fish overboard, and swam ashore with them. The banks were low, but they must have been clever fellows to get heavy pike ashore as they did.

Here, had I a proper regard for dramatic effect, my story should, I suppose, end, but there are still some curious, but perfectly true, incidents to be told concerning those rats.

All went well until I bought a sack of potatoes

which, for lack of room below, was kept on deck for a few days. The very next morning after I made my purchase, Pat came and said that the "divil had been among the piaties" (Irishmen do not say "praties," so far as my experience goes). Half a dozen of them had been rolled out of the sack on to the deck, and were more or less gnawed. This was proof positive that rats were the visitors. I had up to that time some little difficulty in believing that we had been boarded, for no portion of the yacht—no cable—or chain, was touching the bank, so that to reach us the rats would have to swim out some yards and then climb up the anchor chain.

I bought a rat-trap.

A rat did not die that night, nor the next. The trap, baited with a piece of fat bacon, was set on deck, just over my head. Not long after I had turned in I heard something moving about. Perhaps it will hardly be believed, but the pattering of a rat's feet was plainly and unmistakeably audible. Of course, the roof of our cabin was not quite so thick as the floor of a Westminster flat, and consisted merely of the deck planks. Well, I heard a rat. He seemed to come up to the trap and linger about it for a few seconds, as if considering the quality of the bacon. Then he trotted off, and a minute later had a potato out of the sack and was rolling it along the deck. Then other rats came on board, and, after considering the bacon, turned their attention to the "piaties."

It was really very annoying. Both Pat and I laid awake for hours, expecting every moment to hear the snap of the trap. But not a bit of it, the rats would have nothing to say to bacon, but revelled among potatoes.* Finally, to get a little sleep, I fired a rifle out of the window. Splash! Splash! Splash! Splash! Four rats had taken headers overboard. I turned over, and was just beginning to lose myself pleasantly, when there was again a pattering overhead. Those moonlighters had come back! I fired another shot, and they took headers as before. Ere they returned (if they did) I was asleep.

We counted the mangled remains of twenty-two potatoes the next morning.

After this experience I tried sliced tuber as bait, putting the sack below. About eleven o'clock that night, the rats, having come on board, held a lengthy council of war round the trap. Meanwhile I went to sleep, leaving them considering, and nothing of importance transpired.

The matter was getting serious. The rats laughed at us, and, which was worse, kept us awake at night, and were getting so used to the report of the rifle that, so far as I could make out, one or two were beginning to stop on board after I fired.

I took counsel with an aged Irishman. Rats were "mortual cunning," said he, and if there was "the scent of a man's eyebrow on the trap" none of the vermin would take the bait. I was quite sure the trap had not been scented with any eyebrows, but took the precaution of washing it well, and only handling it

---

* Professional rat-catchers do not usually bait traps, but set them in the runs.

c*

while wearing gloves which had been smeared with bacon fat. It was rubbed well and baited with the same excellent substance. If ever man deserved to catch a rat, I did.

On the night that the trap was so carefully perfumed and otherwise rendered attractive, the moon was full, and gave so brilliant a light that we could have read small print out of doors long after sunset. It so happened that a solitary rat paid us a visit before I turned in, and amused himself by running to and fro across the streak of light which spread over the deck from the port-hole in the booby hatch. It was amusing to hear him gently approach the port-hole, and hesitate. After due deliberation he doubtless made up his mind to risk the dangers of the lighted deck and scuttled across the illuminated planks at topmost speed. This performance he repeated many times, paying no attention whatever to the trap until the lights were put out; then, and not till then, he came to consider the bacon.

He was soon joined by one or two more rats, who pattered round and about the bacon-scented affair for hours, now and again leaving it for a few minutes. The anxiety to us in the cabin was something fearful, for a rat was to die before sunrise, and we hoped to keep awake to see it.

Towards the small hours of the morning the excitement gave way to monotony, and we slept.

Snap! Rattle! Squeak! Squeak! Clank! Clank! Squeak! Clank!

I sprung out of my berth, seized a stick, and, without waiting to don any clothing, rushed on deck. A "moonlighter" was in the trap, but, so far as I could make out, was held only by a little piece of skin, and there seemed every chance of his getting away. I aimed a valiant blow at him, but, being more asleep than awake, hit the trap and jerked him out of it.

Then, as reporters say, followed a scene of the most exciting description. The animal bolted between my legs to the other end of the deck, but took no advantage of the splendid opportunity I had given him of a good bite at my bare ankles.

"Hooroo!" cried that villain of a Pat, who, with his head just out of the fore hatch-hole, was enjoying the affair immensely. Why the rat, having reached the stern, did not jump overboard I do not know, but he suddenly turned and rushed past me in the direction of my man, who disappeared like a harlequin through a trap door.

It was a fine scene—my scantily clad self chasing the little robber over the frosted deck by the light of the moon. My blood boiled. I understood then how men felt when charging in battle. My enemy should die; neither his wit nor his legs should save him. Four times did I vainly strike the deck with my stick, and then, remembering that to shoot a flying bird one has to aim forward, I tried the same tactics with this running rat, and gave him a deadly blow.

That fellow must have been the leader, chief adviser, Attorney-General, Prime Minister, Home Secretary,

Poobbah, or what you will, of all the rats in the neighbourhood, for after slaying him the wisdom of the others seemed to have departed, and we had no difficulty in killing numbers of his comrades. Besides, as time went on, we became learned in rat catching. Some nights we covered the trap with a cabbage leaf, and the rats unsuspectingly walking on the leaf, looking for some highly scented bait, met their fate. At other times we melted some tallow on the pan of the trap, and, while it was still moist, stuck a piece of tissue paper on it large enough to cover the whole apparatus. Any rats rambling over the paper in the direction of the tallow, sooner or later touched the pan, and those deadly teeth snapped to.

But never after that night was there occasion for me to wildly chase rats about the deck by moonlight.*

Just before leaving the river I paid a visit to O'Brien's fortress, and asked my two constabulary friends if they discovered anything concerning that mysterious affair of the pike. They modestly said that they had not found out much, though they had been making inquiries; but they believed *they now had a clue.*

"Moonlighters?" I gravely suggested.

"Well, we think so," answered one of them, without hesitation.

"I'm sure of it," said I.

---

* Our moonlight friends, or enemies, as you will, were not voles or water rats, but the common brown Asiatic rats, which haunt town and country alike. Hordes of them tramp the land, taking up their abode in hedgerows, ricks, houses, barns, by rivers; in short, wherever there is food. They swim almost as well as any vole, and are as courageous as they are cunning.—J. B.

In Clonoolia Bay.

"*The Macedonians who live on the banks of the river Astreus, are in the habit of catching a particular fish in that river by means of a fly called hippurus. A very singular insect it is; bold and troublesome like all its kind, in size a hornet, marked like a wasp, and buzzing like a bee. These flies are the prey of certain speckled fish, which no sooner see them settling on the water than they glide gently beneath, and, before the hippurus is aware, snap at and carry him as suddenly under the water as an eagle will seize and bear aloft a goose from a farmyard, or a wolf take a sheep from its fold.*"

ÆLIAN.

"*The great month of the year, for the bungler, is May
And his fly the green drake—if 'tis out, that's to say,
Then the trout catch themselves, so insatiate their lust,
And success is no question of* may, *but of* must."

COTSWOLD ISYS.

CHAPTER III.

IN CLONOOLIA BAY.

On many of the large Irish lakes, the only legitimate methods of angling for trout are trolling in the early spring, and dapping with the green Drake, better known in England as the Mayfly, in May and June. No portion of the many months I spent on Lough Derg was more pleasant than the period during which both fish and birds revelled in their annual banquet on Ephemera vulgaris. Casting in the usual way with the artificial fly seemed next to useless, and this may be owing not to scarcity of the trout, but to their knowledge— by no means inconsiderable—of the many varieties of flies which are dragged over the lake twenty and thirty at a time, by persons fishing with otters and cross lines. On cross lines the trout hook themselves or not at all; consequently, for one that is caught, many are pricked, and the result is a very natural distrust by the fish of anything composed of fur and feathers.

I have so far described only wintry and autumnal scenes and adventures. Let snow and ice be forgotten for awhile in favour of a certain spring and early summer, when our floating abode was moored close to Mount

Shannon, in a charming and secluded portion of the lake called Clonoolia Bay. This was, indeed, almost a separate lake, as a prettily-wooded island with rocky shores, the breeding place of many kinds of water birds, stretched across the front of the bay, shutting it off from the big lake, and only leaving two narrow, rocky, and somewhat dangerous channels through which yachts could, but rarely did, enter. Into this little bay flowed two small streams, near the butts (*Anglicé* mouths) of which I caught many good trout early in the season. Along one side ran a bank, partly covered with yellow gorse; on the other, a small pine wood, stretching out along a rocky point, on which, more often than not, a solitary heron might be seen standing motionless, and apparently —but only apparently—asleep. Two small clusters of rocks bearing a bush or two showed above the surface in one corner of the bay, and were a favourite resting-place for plover in the evening, while along the side nearest the pine wood grew a large bed of reeds. On a sandy shallow between the reed bed and the shore rudd and small perch disported themselves in the hot days of summer.

The surrounding country was for a mile or two wooded and undulating, with here and there cottages, looking picturesque enough, but many of which to my knowledge were squalid and wretched habitations. In the distance rose hills covered with purple heather, where, before Land League hunts came into vogue, grouse abounded. These moorland summits were our barometer when the wind was north-westerly, for a collection of cloud around them was a sure sign of the sharp squall which would shortly come dashing down on to the lake.

It has been said that "prospects, however lovely, may be viewed till half their beauties fade," but the beauties of Clonoolia Bay never palled upon me, and I was so enchanted with the place that I missed a good deal of the Mayfly fishing by remaining there the greater portion of the summer. I should explain that the Mayfly makes its appearance first—usually early in May—at the head of the lake, near the little town of Portumna, the reason doubtless being that the water there is shallower than elsewhere, and gets heated more quickly by the spring sun than where it is deeper. Anglers, who wish to make the most of the drake season, therefore commence their fishing at Portumna, then shift their quarters to Dromineer, Mount Shannon, and Killaloe respectively. At the latter place dapping may be practised with success for at least a fortnight after the rise of fly is over at Mount Shannon. Turning to my diary I see that the fly first made its appearance in Clonoolia Bay about May 25, and went off about June 20. From that time until July 5 the fishing was good in the neighbourhood of Killaloe, a place which has the great advantage of affording excellent night fishing for trout in the river when the lake trout fishing is over. The weekly reports in *The Field* of the salmon fishing speak for themselves. There is also good accommodation for anglers—two hotels, The Royal and the Shannon View, and comfortable lodgings kept by Mrs. Grace, Mr. Hurley and others. At Mount Shannon is a small hotel where anglers do much resort during the green drake carnival.

There can hardly be more enjoyable fishing than drifting with a light breeze on a warm June evening, dapping for trout on some beautiful piece of water such as Clonoolia Bay. A lazy way of catching trout, perhaps, but only lazy until a fish is hooked, when, if he be of any size, the sport is capital owing to the necessary fineness of the tackle. As a rule I used a 13-foot cane rod, not too stiff, though one of 16 feet would have answered the purpose better. For winch nothing is better than the Nottingham pattern with a light check, the line being of fine undressed twisted silk—a trifle stouter than I would use for chub fishing in the Nottingham style on the Thames. If these light lines are used there is no occasion for the old-fashioned skein of floss silk which was formerly added to the line as a sort of sail to catch the wind. A yard or two of fine drawn gut, and a hook, a round bend No. 5, or a little larger completes the simple but necessary tackle. Occasionally two hooks are preferred, one whipped above the other, Stewart fashion. In this case a fly is put on each hook. A good sized basket with a lid is required to contain the flies; and a small aquarium net, wherewith to pick up green drakes that float by, and so keep up the stock in the basket, I found very useful.

Collecting the flies was always one of the troubles of the day, more especially as my man Paddy (Paddys are by no means so numerous in Ireland as is generally supposed), though a keen, clever fisherman and good fellow, was not a too early riser. The windward side of the bay was one of the best hunting grounds, and among the stones which lined that shore were generally to be found some dozens of flies which had drifted across the water, and escaped in marvellous manner from both trout and birds. But these flies were not the best. The fattest and freshest were to be found on the leeward side of bushes fringing the lake. The greenest and largest were the most killing. The dark grey flies were of little use; nor would the trout look at a bright green fly, in shape like a Mayfly, but smaller and greener, which rejoices in the name of Yellow Sally. Paddy declared they were bitter.

During the first three or four days of the flies' appearance the trout will not rise. The reason of this is, I believe, that they feed almost exclusively on the larvæ, or immature flies, which they find on the bottom or ascending to the surface. Some professional eel-catchers, of whom more anon, told me that they take very few eels on their lines during the same period, and those they do catch are almost bursting with immature Mayflies; indeed, they showed me some eels with distended bellies, which I cut open, and found the statement of the men to be perfectly true.

Just at that period of the year both birds and fish seemed to live almost exclusively on the unfortunate Mayfly. Rising early one morning, I put my head cautiously through the hatchway and looked out. Trout were rising in all directions; everywhere flies were coming to the surface of the water, and escaping from their shells only to be swallowed by fish or swifts. An old merganser and a number of downy little ones were close to the yacht, apparently feeding on the unfortunate green

"I SAILED TO KILLALOE."

drakes, while along the shore were numbers of ducks, rooks, seagulls, terns, and other birds eagerly pouncing on the dainty morsels as they were blown towards them.

Early in the day I sailed to Killaloe (which boasted of two, if not three, shops) to replenish our larder, which was getting low, and left instructions with Paddy to have a fine lot of flies collected by my return. Of course, he had nothing of the kind, but the water was simply covered with the delicate little creatures, so that before long we had more than we required. It was about six o'clock when we began fishing. Paddy rowed me up to the point by the pine wood, turned the boat broadside to the wind, which was, as usual in Ireland, westerly, and we began our first drift. The breeze, which had been fresh all day, had softened considerably, and was just as a wind should be—enough of it to carry out the fly, but not sufficient to cause the boat to drift fast.

The style of fishing of which I am writing is wrongly termed dapping, for the perfection of it is not to dap the fly, but to let it rest lightly on the water and be carried along by the wind. A beginner is forced to let a few inches of gut lie on the water, but a practised hand will keep the fly and nothing more on the surface, and, however strong the wind, half a gale excepted, will not suffer it to rise for even a second. If the wind freshens a little, the point of the rod is lowered and the fly is kept down; if it falls, the point of the rod should be raised to keep the slackened gut from falling on the water. Whether one or more flies are used, and how they should be put on the hook, so far as my experience goes, matters little. Lake trout do not object to a natural Mayfly, even if standing on its head.

We commenced our drift, sitting one in the stem and

the other in the stern, it being important to trim the boat carefully, or otherwise she would not keep broadside on to the wind. It was a perfect fishing evening, and trout were rising freely all round us, but not exactly in our course, and we drifted nearly across the bay without a rise, when, just as my man was putting out a scull to keep us off the rocks of the shore opposite to that from which we had started, a gleam of golden yellow shone in the water, my line tightened, the reel gave forth music delicious to the angler's ear, and I knew I was fast in a good trout. I was awkwardly situated, for the fish was hemmed in between the boat and the shore. However, Paddy very skilfully punted the boat away from the rocks, which gave me a fair chance with a handsome and beautifully conditioned gillaroo of $4\frac{1}{4}$lb.

"Gillaroo" is a word which is likely to puzzle our general readers and not a few anglers, suffice it to say here, that it spells trout. For the benefit of those who take an interest in matters piscatorial I have dealt with these interesting fish in chapter six, which is more or less devoted to the slaying of gillaroos.

After killing this fine fish Paddy advised that the bay should be given a rest, so we rowed outside and took several drifts over the rocky shallows which stretch out for some distance on the south side of Cribby Island.

We were now on the open lake which stretched away for miles to the west, east, and south. To the eastward the view up the lake was closed by Ilanmore, or big island, and the Carrigeen Islands. These latter and Cribby always hold a pleasant place in my memory as having furnished me with the background and scenery for a little fairy legend of the Shannon—the first piece of book work which I ever perpetrated. The man who was rowing me on the evening I am describing, figured in the story as one Andy who was changed into a fairy and made desperate love to by a fairy spinster of uncertain age. This to his great distraction, as he had a wife and family at Mount Shannon. But all fairy tales have to end happily, so of course Andy was restored to his proper shape and his sorrowing wife and children. Little did honest Paddy think as we drifted over the shoals around Cribby that he would some day be the hero of a fairy booklet.

The open lake only yielded us a solitary trout of about a pound and a half, for the fish were certainly less numerous on the more exposed shores than in the sheltered portion between the mainland and the numerous islands, so at the end of an hour we returned to Clonoolia Bay and found the fish rising as merrily as ever.

Our first drift produced two trout of about three-quarters of a pound each; then followed a drift without a fish, though my hook was cleverly bared several times. After that we tried a very favourite corner of mine, where huge rocks rise nearly to the surface and the water is deep. As a rule, Paddy always objected to any suggestion coming from me as to the place where we should fish; but the four-pounder had evidently mollified him, for, in reply to my direction to row over to Page's Point, he exclaimed:

"I will ; why wouldn't I? and six times!"

However, he only did it once, and the result was a slender, silvery fish of 2lb. weight, very different in appearance to the short, thick gillaroo with its golden belly and large spots. Shortly after this, anyone passing by the yacht might have noticed a pleasant fragrance in the air, and, on casting an eye down the fore hatchway, would have seen the writer carefully tending some half-dozen oval pieces of fish of a delicate pink adorned with creamy curd, round which the golden butter frizzled. Gillaroo cutlets make a princely dish, my friends.

Among the Clare Hills.

"*There is a multiplicity of gentlemen's seats between Lup's Head and Limerick, delightfully situated on the Rivers Shannon and Fergus. Their charming prospect and elegant improvements richly merit the attention of the curious.*"

"A Short Tour, or, an Impartial and Accurate Description of the County of Clare." A.D. 1780.

"*Hope in my heart; health in the air,
The freshness of morning everywhere,
Pleasure before, and care behind,
I tramp to the river with gleesome mind,
And with brotherly love to all mankind!
And the tramp of my eager feet doth say
I wonder, I wonder what luck to-day!*"

Cotswold Isys.

CHAPTER IV.

AMONG THE CLARE HILLS.

My very first experience of anything approaching wild life in Ireland was gained during a visit to the country house of an Irish Judge, father of my old college friend, Harry H. The house was situated on a slope of the Clare Hills, not far from Kildysart, and possessed a magnificent outlook over the estuary of the Shannon, which, even these many miles from its mouth, is a considerably larger expanse of water than Lough Derg.

My most kind and hospitable hosts could offer their friends pretty well everything that the heart of the sportsman could desire, from shooting snipe down to oyster-picking on the rocks. There was an old hooker lying in a creek, and I longed to go to sea in her, but was deterred by the fact that the inevitable Irish hole in the bottom was unrepaired, save for a sod of turf which had saved Harry and his friends from destruction on some previous occasions. But we had the gandola, a flat-bottomed craft bearing a slight resemblance to the Venetian vessel of almost the same name, and designed to be slid over the "slob," or mud banks, which were exposed at low water. It was a novel experience to sit in this curious craft and be sent spinning down the incline of mud and dash into the water at ever so many miles an hour. The whole proceeding was joyous and exhilarating, and anticipated Captain Boyton's watershute at the Earl's Court Exhibition by several years. But if a landing had to be made before high water, and that same gandola had to be pushed up the muddy banks by perspiring individuals with their shoes and stockings off and trousers turned up to the knee, who sank in two feet of mud at every step, the labour required was Herculean, and the pace and proceedings generally of the most funereal and doleful description. On this same slob we sometimes saw the marks where a sole, plaice, or flounder had been resting, and when at high water the seine was run out and hauled in, it generally contained some fish worth the having.

Among other new sensations, I had the pleasure of catching my first char in a fine sheet of water known as Gort Glas, which means in English, Green Garden. It was a pretty fish, but less red on the belly than other char I have caught elsewhere. I took his photograph, and the result may be seen on the next page.

I had tried nearly all the waters on the domain except one particular little lake high up among the hills, which was Harry's favourite fishing ground. This I had not yet visited, for, being distant, to obtain more than an hour or two's fishing on it during the day was impossible, unless one was provided with a tent and slept out on the bog. A camp by the side of this lake

among the Clare Hills was a part of the programme which my kind friends had planned for my benefit. One spring morning, therefore, a young larch tree was felled to provide a new tent pole, sundry arrangements were made with the cook, and very early the following day the tent and other impedimenta was dispatched to the lake in what was called the ass-cart, we following a little later in the day on the outside car.

Harry had been telling me some wild stories of otters which haunted his lake in great numbers, and for a while I became possessed with a most ardent longing to distinguish myself by slaying some of them. Having no proper traps I obtained with great difficulty from Ennis a coil of soft wire with which to ensnare them, but whether otters ever have been or ever will be ensnared with wire I have no knowledge.

The only result of my wire was to render myself an object of great suspicion to the sergeant in command of the little black and white constabulary station in the nearest village. Notwithstanding the great store I set upon it I very nearly left the coil behind, and most of our luggage having gone on, and the well of the car being full to overflowing, I had to hold my wire, and for convenience put my arm through the coil and pushed it up well above my elbow. Then we happened upon the sergeant, who was standing by the roadside as we turned from the valley towards the moorland above us. He saluted Harry H. and fixed his baleful eye upon my arm, which was encircled with the wire, and stood in the middle of the road watching us until we were out of sight. He must have next struck up over the moorland, and as the road was a long winding one, and we were going at a walking pace, was able to cut us off at another turning. To our surprise he reappeared, and still more intently than before regarded the barbaric ornament on my arm, but said no word. Harry and I discussed the man's strange behaviour, but could make nothing of it. A mile further, he burst upon us a third time, very much blown now and out of breath, and stared so fixedly at my arm that it became perfectly clear the wire was the great attraction; and I am sorry to say that there is nothing more interesting to relate concerning either the coil or the man. The wire did not even catch an otter, for whether we were too fully occupied with the trout, or I was satisfied with having unintentionally bamboozled a fine, upstanding, young sergeant of the R.I.C. I cannot say; however that may be, no noose was set and the marauding otters were left in peace.

After the third visit from the sergeant the horse broke into a trot and we soon found ourselves some hundreds of feet above the Shannon, the estuary of which noble river, several miles in width, could be seen sparkling in the sunlight, winding between the hills of Clare and Kerry, flowing westwards towards the Atlantic. Higher still, and we caught a glimpse of the sea, and, when the good little Irish horse stopped to recover his wind, could hear the distant thundering of mighty breakers. On all sides stretched far away great tracts of bog and moorland. Here and there was the stone-built cottage of a herd, chimneyless, gardenless, treeless, flowerless. On the slope of a hill sheltered from the westerly gales by a row of trees, was one small farm-house. For miles we saw no human being, except a lad leading a sleek donkey bearing panniers, loaded with peat from the adjacent bog.

"A SLEEK DONKEY, BEARING PANNIERS LOADED WITH PEAT."

We turned out of our way here to pay a visit to one of the curiosities of the district, a centenarian named Padneen Honan, who lived with his daughter in a village among the hills. I had my camera with me and photographed the old man as he might be seen sitting at work any summer's day making baskets outside his cabin, with his daughter spinning by his side.

As to that particular photograph there is rather a curious history. We had for about an hour to leave the car in charge of some peasants, and gave them strict injunctions not to open any of the photographic apparatus which they took into the house for fear of rain. The result, of course, was that they did open the slides to see what was inside the machine, and as I unfortunately deferred the development of the plates until almost the last day of my visit, it was then too late to repair the damage, for all the action of the chemical produced was one plain sheet of black, neither Padneen, daughter, dog, nor spinning-wheel being anywhere visible.

I lamented greatly over this affair, because the old man was one of the few Irishmen left in the district who still wore knee-breeches and the old cut-away coat. Spinning-wheels, too, had become uncommon, and altogether I regarded the picture as a notable one. Harry H. was equally sorry, because Hoonan was one of his father's tenants for whom they had a great regard, while being over a hundred, in the nature of things he could not live much longer, and a photograph of him would possess great interest to the family. Suddenly I had an inspiration.

"I will give you a lesson in photography to-night." said I, "and the next time you go up in the hells you shall photograph the man yourself."

"ONE OF THE FEW IRISHMEN LEFT IN THE DISTRICT WHO STILL WORE KNEE-BREECHES."

My friend had never taken a photograph before and knew nothing of the manipulation of the camera, but he not only learnt the lesson I gave him so well that he went up the hills and posed the figures correctly, and accurately exposed the plate, but on his return home actually developed it and produced the illustration which is shown on the opposite page. I doubt if there was ever a better first photograph produced, but then Harry is cleverer and more painstaking than most men.

While dealing with matters photographic I may tell the story of how I married two people in camera as may be seen on the frontispiece. I was driving to the upper waters of a moorland river, when there crawled out of a curious little cabin by the roadside a very aged crone, whom I immediately became fired with a desire to photograph. The coachman happened to know her slightly, and was an Irishman, so I thought it best to send him to ask her gracious permission to put her in a picture. She seemed greatly puzzled to know why anyone should want her portrait, and thought there must be something bad in it, for, as she truly said, it was not as if she was "a young girl whose picture the gentleman might like to have by him"! However, O'Brien, the coachman, explained that I had a penchant for photographs of old women, and having grasped this fact, she very reluctantly consented to sit on a stone outside her cottage door for a minute or two. Just as I had the camera arranged and the lens ready to be uncapped, it so happened that there came strolling down the road one of the finest-looking peasants I ever saw in Ireland, or indeed anywhere else. Harvest had commenced and a scythe was over his shoulder.

"If I could only get the two of them," thought I, "this would indeed be a good day's work." So I somewhat abruptly stopped him with, "See here, Pat, we're just making a picture and you'll look fine in it. Come and stand there now, and be photographed!"

"Indeed an' I will," he said, and the old woman, who was half blind, not noticing it, he stood by her side just as you may see him in the picture.

The shutter was instantly set, and in four seconds the first step had been taken in the preparation of a most damning piece of evidence against this worthy couple, presuming either of their mates required to get a divorce, but I now remember, by the way, that the old woman was a widow. Widow or no, never was an old woman more angry in her life than this one when she found she had been photographed with this fine old fellow by her side. I called on her a week later with the object of giving her a print of the photograph, and she most rudely and ungratefully slammed the door in my face and would not let me put foot inside the cottage. On the whole, looking at the two heads, it appears that the old man had the greatest grievance.

* * * * *

Padneen photographed, the grey horse was put between the shafts, and we hurried on towards our camping ground. We were all impatience, for in most of the valleys were small lakes, and on them a curl, which boded well for our sport in the afternoon.

Still higher, and we lost sight of cottage and farm; all around us was bare moorland. I was beginning to wonder where the trout of which we were in search could be found, when the car stopped, and looking over a bank, there in a hollow on the top of the hill, not fifty yards away, was a little lake.

Lough Creina, so let me call it, is a lovely piece of water, between fifteen and twenty acres in extent, and lies, though many feet above sea level, at the foot of a flat-topped heather-clad mountain called Slieve or Mount Callan. The northern shore of the lake, and doubtless also the bottom on that side, is rocky. On the southern shore, where grow water lilies and a few reeds, a little brook runs *out* of the lake into which no visible stream flows, and, passing over many a gravelly shallow and tiny fall, wanders away through the bogs into some larger rivulet, which doubtless ultimately discharges itself into the Shannon estuary. It was *down* this stream that the lake trout would retire to spawn in winter time, reversing thereby the natural and well-known order of things, for other trout usually head *up* stream in the late autumn; these fish were undoubtedly peculiar, but then they had no choice. Down stream they must go, or else stick to the lake, in which spawning was "love's labour lost."

Skirting the shore nearest the road was a slope of bright green turf, and on this stood a patient jennet between the shafts of the cart which had brought up a bell tent, the larch tree tent-pole, and the various other requirements of a camper-out.

I had hardly leapt from the car before I saw a fish rise, and then another and another; but, however impatient we might be to get on the water, certain necessary things had to be done. In the first place there was a hole in the boat, which had to be patched up with brown paper and tar, to say nothing of various little caulkings which were absolutely needful before we could venture in her on the rippling water. Then the tent had to be pitched, and a trench dug round it; moreover, before the dew began to fall, it was necessary to gather many armfuls of fragrant heather with which to make our bed. While these things were doing, I endeavoured to excavate a scientific fireplace in the side of a bank, building a chimney thereto of much architectural beauty with sods of turf.

But all things must have an end, and in the course of an hour or so our preparations were complete, and we were afloat, intent upon catching trout for supper. Rowing up to the westward, we drifted back along the edge of a small reed-bed. The wind had now fallen somewhat, and we needed no stone to check the pace of our little craft. The trout were plentiful, but rose rather short. My friend N. killed the first fish, which, for its size, fought magnificently, almost as much out of the water as in it. At the end of two or three minutes the poor thing left the water for good, and was knocked on the head. Then my turn came, and I had the pleasure of playing one of the gamest trout—sea-trout excepted—which have ever risen to my fly. I have often thought, when killing a fish in a more or less weedy chalk stream, that many would be the smashes of tackle and deep the lamentations of Hampshire anglers, if the trout of the South of England at all approached these little fellows of the lake in strength and agility. It is not an exaggeration to say that the $\frac{1}{4}$lb. fish in that and some other lakes I could mention, are every bit as strong as chalk-stream fish of double their size.

The next drift was towards the rocky shore, where weeds and mud were not, and I noticed that, whereas the trout caught by the reeds were golden-bellied and generally warm in colour, those by the rocks were silver-bellied, with very dark backs and steely-blue sides. This is the rule rather than the exception in most streams and lakes.

As the short spring day closed in, the wind died away, the lake calmed down, and the trout, though they continued to break the surface, became uncatchable. So we made our way to the tent and feasted on fried trout, cold beef, and whisky—all very good things.

Here let me confess that my scientifically-constructed fireplace in the side of the hill proved a dismal failure, the chimney suffering greatly from that complaint termed by builders "down draught." One reason for this, doubtless, was that I had dug into a subterranean river which flowed down from the back of the fireplace and under the big stone which did duty for hearth. Later on in the evening we managed to get up a big fire, and minded little that the flames flared out in front instead of going up the chimney, for they warmed us the more, and the night was intensely cold. So cold was it, indeed, that the following morning I found my sponge frozen. This was really remarkable, for it had been left in a sponge bag, which was in a Gladstone bag, all being in the tent in which a mineral oil lamp was kept alight until sunrise.

Ours was not the only fire on the mountain that night, as, caring little for the fact that the grouse had recently nested, certain peasants set light to the heather on many of the hills. The sight was a fine one, but we felt sad on account of the poor birds which were being roasted, not only before their time, but alive.

It was not cockcrow or the gleams of the rising sun that awoke me the following morning at daybreak, but the uncouth voices of two men just outside the tent, who were carrying on an animated conversation in Irish or Erse, a language of which I knew nothing.

We were in a wild place, and visions of moonlighters and other noxious things sprang into my mind. I touched Harry, who was sleeping soundly, and begged him to heed the possible danger in which we were placed. It was some minutes before he was sufficiently awake to make out what the men were saying, and then, turning to me with a queer look, half-crusty at being woke up so early, half-amused at what he had heard, quietly remarked that the moonlighters were merely two "bhoys" criticising my scientific fireplace.

"And what do they think of it?" asked I.

"I won't hurt your feelings, old man, by telling you," replied Harry, rolling off the heather bed, and proceeding to dress.

As soon as I had my boots on I kicked down the turf chimney, and generally demolished my moorland grate.

A surprise was in store for us outside the tent. In a little hollow formed by three big stones a fire burned brightly. On the fire a kettle sang merrily, and close to the door of the tent stood a can of rich goat's milk. Where was the good fairy who had done these things? I queried; but Harry was mysterious, and the most I could get from him was that sooner or later he would introduce me to her.

By the time we had cooked and eaten our breakfasts and (odious operation) washed the frying-pan and other things, the sun was high in the heavens. The sky was cloudless, and there was not the faintest breath of air to ruffle the surface of the lake. We attempted to catch a trout, but our only chance was to cast right into the ripples made by rising fish. This was a delicate and tedious affair, which we soon tired of and gave up.

"Come and see the good fairy," said Harry, and we went.

In a hollow not two hundred yards from our tent we came to a cabin which I had not hitherto seen, and entering, saw dimly through the smoke an aged woman seated with a pipe in her mouth by the side of a turf fire. She was dark and looked smoke-dried (there was no chimney), but had a kindly, pleasant face. She welcomed us warmly, and Harry explained that, despite her appearance, she was the good fairy who had so thoughtfully lit the fire for us in the morning.

After the introduction, conversation languished, as Mrs. O'Callaghan had but little English; but there was time to notice that the cottage consisted of two rooms, and that in the larger one, where our hostess was sitting, a cow had apparently passed the night. A pig looked in at the door, but, seeing us, gave a grunt and turned away. A chicken which had laid an egg in the corner of the room went out clucking and much elated. A nanny-goat wandered in and stared at us in great amazement; but I think I was the more amazed of the two. In the cottage dwelt three generations of humans, Mrs. O'Callaghan and her husband, their son, and their son's children. How many families there were of the lower orders of animal life I did not ascertain with accuracy. It is worth placing on record that O'Callaghan had no rent to pay, his cottage and the grass for a cow being given him for certain services he rendered as herd.

Some years later I took the opportunity of another visit to Clare to photograph the O'Callaghan's cabin, but alas! (from a picturesque point of view) the plasterer and whitewasher and thatcher had been at work, and even a bricklayer had been employed to erect a chimney, the result being the extremely neat cottage shown in the illustration. Down the valley to the right of the cottage, in the distance, there is Lough Creina, which is the first view one gets of it driving up the moorland road. I never long so much for photography in colours to be an established fact as when looking over these photographs

LOUGH CREINA AND THE O'CALLAGHAN'S CABIN.

of Irish scenery, for the undulating moorland which possesses the most lovely colouring, ever changing with the shifting light, is all too inadequately portrayed in various shades of one tone. Looking at the picture, I see coming up the valley, though very small in the distance, Harry himself and two of the O'Callaghan's

E *

gossoons carrying the sculls of the old dinghy to place them in the cottage, in the best room of which, when we drove to the lake, we used to stable the horse. This was no great outrage, for it merely occupied the place which appertained to the cow in the winter time.

Our visit to the worthy dame over, we returned to the lake, but found matters there as hopeless as before, so decided to walk to Miltown Malbay, some fourteen miles distant.

Here let me mention that since then I have found by experience that when in lake fishing the weather is as I have described, the trout, if feeding, can sometimes be caught by allowing the fly to sink several feet, and then drawing it slowly up to the surface. A dry fly cast deftly into the circles caused by rising fish will also help to make up a few brace under such conditions as these.

The first four miles of our walk was over the bog, and hard work it was in the broiling sun, which scorched us up, and caused much epidermic peeling the following day. On the way we passed a large lake, along the shores of which thousands of small trout were repeatedly rising. The margin of the water was literally rippling with them. Here Harry told me that by fishing with several flies an unheard-of number of trout might be caught in a day, but as regards their weight the less said the better.

Soon after striking the high road a ridiculous thing occurred. We were anxious to leave our woollen "sweaters" at a cottage, but the girl who came to the door, and who could speak but little English, thought we were pedlars, and for some time was most energetic in her assurances that she didn't "want any at all, at all." On the door of each cabin and cottage we passed was a large cross in what looked like red paint—some religious observance, I suppose, connected perhaps with the season of Lent or Easter, which was not long past. Sometimes this cross is placed on the door to avert or defeat bad luck, as when illness has come upon the family or cattle have died.

Miltown Malbay I found to be a very uninteresting place, containing many interesting people. In the summer time the country people come down here to the sea for medicinal rows, rendered more effective by drinks of sea water. It must be exciting work riding over Atlantic billows in the frail craft, which consist of a light framework covered with canvas. We had no time to go to the seashore, but I had the satisfaction of seeing the Irishman as he is still represented in *Punch* and on the stage, but minus his blackthorn. The ancient dress is very little worn now, except by old men, such as our centenarian, in remote districts.

We started on our walk back to the tent in what we thought was good time, but as we went along I found Harry getting very anxious; and when he explained that if night came on while we were on the bog we should have to stop wherever we might be, I shared his anxiety. Harry's fears proved by no means groundless, for at sunset we were still some distance from the tent, and it was only by running over the bog for the last mile—a run which we, of course, thoroughly appreciated after our long walk and the hot exhausting day—that we managed to get off the treacherous ground before nightfall. There are bogs and bogs. Some are comparatively safe, others are dangerous even in the daylight. Parts of the one we crossed were very bad indeed.

While I prepared supper, Harry went out in the boat and managed to get a brace of fish, a useful addition to our stock of food, which was low. A nasty, smoky, lurid sunset had boded bad weather, and before we turned in my friend was careful to hammer in the tent pegs and tighten the ropes. The precaution was a wise one, for a little before daybreak there came a furious storm of wind and rain from the west which threatened every moment to tear our tent from the ground. It was one of the worst storms I ever experienced. The wind blew as only it can blow on the hills near the west coast of Ireland, with nothing to check the fury of its passage right across the great Atlantic.

But morning came at last, and soon after breakfast appeared the car which was to take us back to civilisation. On the car was an under-keeper, with whose assistance we managed to launch the dingby and do a little fishing. Though the boat was light, it required two to row her against the fierce wind. There was an extraordinarily great sea on for so small a lake, and our craft began to leak badly. The trout, however, rose well, and we had good sport. I put on, as an experiment, a large black chub fly that happened to be in my book, and found it answer remarkably well in the rough water. At length, however, we were literally blown off the lake, and had to give up fishing, much to my regret, while the fish were still rising.

I might write much more of our doings during those three happy days, the strange people we saw, and the curious traditions connected with the lake; but I will conclude this chapter by telling of a certain attempt to improve the fishing made by Harry's brother in 1872, and the deplorable and unexpected results therefrom. This relation I should say at once may be judiciously skipped by the general reader, being however, serviceable information to owners of lochs, lochans and loughs.

Previously no fault could possibly be found with the quality, or, taking into consideration the size of the lake, the quantity of the fish. Harry told me they were the most handsome trout he had ever seen—thick, deep, beautifully marked with large spots, and flesh—to use the words of the country people—"as red as a coal of fire." They averaged a couple of ounces under the pound, and were much of a size, the largest on record being 1¼lb. The average take would be ten to a dozen fish, over that number a good day, and more than two dozen very exceptional.

As the lake lies high, where flies are scarce, and contains no other fish than trout, the feed is necessarily limited, and the numbers taken were quite as great as could reasonably be expected. But it was thought otherwise, and as every winter a large number of fish when down the brook spawning were killed by the peasants, a dam was placed across the stream just where it leaves the lake. It was a low broad wall of loose stones, through which the water flowed easily, but fish of any size could not pass. There were and still are traces of an older dam at the same place, and there is a tradition among the country people that, some fifty years ago, when it was standing, fish were exceedingly numerous in the lake. The poachers objecting to the new dam, pulled it down. Three times it was rebuilt, and finally allowed to remain.

Now note what followed. The second year after the erection of the dam, a number of small trout, some 2oz. or 3oz. in weight, were caught. Each year these small fish increased greatly in numbers, slightly in size, and the lake became very full of them. In weight they ran from $\frac{1}{4}$lb. to $\frac{1}{2}$lb.; and, if the day were at all favourable, it was an easy matter to kill from two to three dozen. They were thin and half-fed, and not more than two-thirds of the old average weight. In June and July they had spawn in them, which never used to be the case; and Harry told me that once in May he caught a fish which had in it some of the old year's spawn, as well as the new year's in process of development. This, however, strange as it may seem, is not uncommon, as all fish culturists know. There was nothing in the new generation to compensate for the falling off in the old. When the evil effects of the dam were so clearly demonstrated, it was allowed to fall into ruins, and the fish have run down the stream to spawn as in former times, but in quality and size they have not greatly improved, gamely as they play. It is quite possible that the lake now contains more trout than the natural supply of food can support.

I was considerably puzzled as to the course events had taken with regard to this dam. Why should the trout increase in a lake when cut off from their only spawning ground? Yet increased they had beyond any doubt. But I had overlooked the fact that small trout can spawn in small places, and that not only would some few fish probably find their way through the loose stone wall, but also that a tiny streamlet, some eight or ten inches broad, trickled into the lake by the side of our tent—which stream, by the bye, was exceedingly useful in that most odious of all camping-out operations— washing up.

Sir James Gibson Maitland, to whom I mentioned some of the foregoing details, was kind enough to give me an explanation of the matter. Small trout, he said, have been known to breed in drains and springs which are usually included in the statement, "nothing flows into the lake." In Lough Creina the larger fish were prevented from descending the brook, and, though they shed their spawn annually, it could not develop in the lake. The breed was thus carried on by the smaller trout which could make use of spring holes and insignificant drains. Some of them, too, could perhaps get through crevices in the dam. The progeny of youthful trout have been found by experiment at Howietoun to rarely attain a weight of $\frac{1}{2}$lb., and youthful trout being the only propagators of their species in Lough Creina, a race of pigmies was the result. Small, stunted parents produce small, stunted children. Moreover, the progeny of the small trout in former years probably paid a very heavy tax to the stronger and more advanced fry of the larger fish; and this Nature seems to intend, as the larger fish spawn early and their fry are thus ahead of, and in a position to feed on, the fry of the small fish, which spawn late. Below the dam, the fry of the smaller trout, safe from the fry of the larger fish, increased and multiplied, and then ascended into the lake. With regard to the retarded development of spawn, that was due to want of condition caused by overcrowding and insufficient food.

There can be no doubt that the reasons given by Sir James to account for the deterioration of the breed are correct, and there can be equally no doubt that, unless active steps are taken to remove the dwarfs and replace them by well-bred fish, it will be many years before the "thick, deep, beautifully-marked" fish, "averaging a couple of ounces under the pound," a very respectable average, by the bye, in any lake—will again be found in beautiful Lough Creina. There is a moral in all this, and perhaps it is "Let well alone."

Brian Boru's Snipe.

*"There's a twofold sweetness in double pipes;
And a double barrel and double snipes
Give the sportsman a duplicate pleasure."*

HOOD.

Killaloe was formerly noted for great encampments, and famous for its vicinity with Ceanncora. This was the large and royal mansion of Bryan Borovy, and his illustrious Ancestors; this renowned deliverer of his country reigned thirty-six years King of Munster, and twelve years Monarch of Ireland; he fought forty-nine battles against the Danes and their allies, etc.: in most of which he was victorious; the last he fought on Good Friday, April 22nd, 1034, on the Plains of Clontarff, near Dublin, where he fell."

"A SHORT TOUR, OR AN IMPARTIAL AND ACCURATE DESCRIPTION OF THE COUNTY OF CLARE," BY JOHN LLOYD. 1780.

CHAPTER V.

BRIAN BORU'S SNIPE.

Few branches of sport are more uncertain than snipe-shooting. Though there are certain well-known rules concerning their habits, snipe seem to delight in proving that to every rule there is an exception, and to some many. In hard weather, as every snipe-shooter knows, the birds usually haunt the warmer springs of the valleys; but I have sometimes found these spots deserted during fairly severe frosts, and the little creatures lying out on the higher moorlands among the heather, where there was apparently no food for them, and this when snow was on the ground. There is no end to their vagaries.

One cold November morning I remember fruitlessly walking certain marshes bordering a large lough—a bit of country which ought to have abounded, and usually did abound, with snipe, many of them Irish-bred birds. In the afternoon I fished, and, to my astonishment, put up two wisps, five or six birds in each, from rocky islets which bore no grass or verdure of any kind, and were each small enough to have gone under my boat's sail.

This happened not more than two hundred yards from the marshes over which in the morning I had shot, or rather walked, without seeing a bird.

Very pleasant recollections come back to me of a singular and really notable day's snipe-shooting I and my old friend D— enjoyed on the borders of the Shannon. The time was winter, not long after Christmas, and an enjoyable cruise of a few weeks' duration, was nearly at an end. Our chief aim and object had been duck and wildfowl generally, but, the weather having been very mild and open, the birds had been shy in the extreme, and our success not very great. We had not yet seen Killaloe and the picturesque portion of the lake which leads down to it; so our host advised us to pay that notable fishing station a visit and kindly offered us a letter of introduction to Mr. P—, a cousin of his, who had some snipe-shooting on certain water-meadows by the river.

"They" (the meadows) "run from Brian Boru's Castle to the village, so you can't mistake them," said Captain S—, adding, "I have never found many birds there, but, with good luck, you ought to pick up two or three couple."

The night following this conversation there was a slight fall of snow, and the glass registered three or four degrees of frost. The next morning the yacht slipped away from her moorings before we had turned out, and, with a beam wind all the way we arrived at Killaloe about eleven o'clock.

As we left the lake and glided into the river's mouth, I noticed on our right some ancient earthworks of curious form. These consisted of a low grass-clad hill, in shape not unlike a sugar-loaf with its top sliced off—the edge of its summit encircled with a ring of tall, well-grown trees. I afterwards found that within the circle was a depression in the ground—a miniature crater. From this curious hill there trended to the

"FROM BRIAN BORU'S CASTLE TO THE VILLAGE."

river's edge a considerable mound which was evidently the work of man in ages long past. Our skipper told us that the hill was all that remained of a stronghold built by the great Brian Boru, and related the following interesting legend of the adjoining earthwork:

Once on a time this illustrious Irish king was greatly troubled by the proceedings of a rival monarch or chieftain whose territory consisted, in a great measure, of lowlying lands bordering the upper Shannon.

"Begor," said Brian one morning at breakfast, "I will build me a big dam from mountain to mountain where the waters of the lough flow into the river, the lough will rise twenty feet, spread all over the counthry, and that schoundrel and his people will be drowned like the rats they are!"

Could Brian's engineers have been equal to such a dam the country would have been flooded for miles around, the area of the lake perhaps been doubled, and the enemy discomfited. But the force of the water was too much for them, and the war had to be carried on by less ingenious methods. In proof of the truth of the legend there is the half-finished dam to be seen to this day, standing out from the site of the old fortress right to the very shores of the lough.

* * * * *

I may here tell another story of a castle on the banks of Lough Derg, on Clanricarde territory, a few miles south of Portumna. During one of the periodic contests between landlord and tenant in the south and west several of these old places were fortified, and with more or less success withstood battering-rams and sieges. This one in particular was blockaded with solid masonry backed by trunks of trees and masses of stone. It was fully provisioned and manned and was deemed impregnable. It seems that until it had been surrendered legal possession could not have been taken of the farm on which it stood.

The newspapers were full of the defence of this ancient Irish chieftain's stronghold, and the affair was the talk of the country. Police in great numbers, and military, assembled at Portumna, and one morning before dawn they started with bailiffs, emergency men, battering-rams, etc., in order to begin evicting at sunrise.

A young man, whom I will call O'Donoghue, went with the attacking army to see the fun, and having inspected the outside of the place with the constabulary inspector, was greatly struck with the strength of the fortifications and wondered how the garrison got in and out. At last he found something like a chimney shaft leading from an external fireplace up to what were once the upper floors, a place doubtless to shoot down household rubbish. Looking up this shaft, he saw a rope hanging down inside it from a kind of trapdoor at the top. He laughingly said he would climb up and pay the garrison a visit, and though strongly dissuaded by the constabulary inspector, on the grounds that there would be a breach of the peace, he clambered up, saying that he was only going as a visitor. With grave misgivings, he pushed open the trapdoor and found inside the castle not a single living being, but great quantities of stones, water and other fluids, potatoes and provisions.

The fact was, the defenders being well aware that the eviction could not legally commence until sunrise, and having no mind to spend the night on the top of a cold, draughty old castle, had been having a good time in the farmhouse hard by. O'Donoghue accordingly shouted down that there was no one in the place, and pulled up the rope.

The next act in this little drama commenced just before the hour of sunrise, when twenty stalwart fellows marched from the farmhouse to garrison their fortress. Their faces and feelings can be imagined when they found the rope pulled up and themselves exposed to the jeers of the emergency men. Immediately after dawn came the sheriff to the door of the castle and demanded who was inside. O'Donoghue replied that he was. He was then asked if he would give up possession peaceably, and he said that so far as he was concerned he would, and he did; and this was the end of the Great Siege.

At one time Ireland was full of small kings or chieftains and the ruins of their castles are very numerous. They are mostly square towers of the type shown in the illustration, which is reproduced from a photograph I took near Ballynacally, in County Clare. But I am wandering far from Killaloe, which, while these stories have been in the telling, the yacht's head has been slowly approaching.

Inside the river, which is here as wide as Henley regatta reach, we were sheltered from the wind by the tall hills towering above us, but there was sufficient impetus on the yacht to carry us right into the reeds, which fringed the banks and were alive with waterhens and coots. Our skipper then went ashore and in the course of half an hour brought us a note from Mr. P—, who wrote that we were quite at liberty to shoot over the water meadows, and wished us good sport.

A few minutes later the yacht's punt was being poled through the reeds by our skipper, and D— and I landed

"THEY ARE MOSTLY SQUARE TOWERS."

on a little green oasis of turf, which was dry compared with the rest of the meadows. In using the word water-meadows I am hardly accurate, for the fields could not be flooded at will, but were rather marshes, which their owner, by cutting deep transverse drains, had been at no small pains to bring into cultivation. Here there was no snow, but there was a little ice among the reeds, and the moorlands and mountains above us were covered with their white winter clothing.

We had not proceeded half a dozen steps before two snipe rose almost at our feet. We had not expected anything quite so soon, but managed to secure one of them; indeed, I rather fancy D— and I both shot it; at any rate, we demonstrated with great clearness that both aimed at the same bird. A few steps further another snipe rose within a couple of yards of D—, who winged it, whilst I, having on a pair of stout "Field" boots, and being therefore independent of the water, acted for the nonce as retriever. The fun, which was fast before, now became furious; and, without dogs, we put up snipe every few yards, often two and sometimes three at once.

Both of us shot abominably. To begin with, the walking was bad—for the field was only a few inches above the river, consequently soft in the extreme; and in turning sharply to shoot birds rising in unexpected places, one foot might remain on a springy tuft of grass, whilst the other would descend to awful depths in the mud.

Snipe-shooting is not, as a rule, easy work to Englishmen, who do not have those opportunities of practice enjoyed by most Irish country gentlemen; but it becomes doubly difficult when the walking is bad or dangerous. I had a further excuse for bad shooting, inasmuch as both barrels of my gun were fully choked. I think it will be generally acknowledged that choke-bores are not desirable weapons for snipe, except in the hands of the most skilled, even though the cartridges are judiciously loaded to scatter, as were mine on that occasion. I must confess, however, that I did not hold my gun particularly straight, and many a snipe "'*scaped* in earnest," as an old writer on shooting jocosely puts it. However, I am not inditing these remarks with the object of glorifying my own shooting deeds—or the reverse—but rather to set on record what was in truth a most remarkable day's snipe shooting, such as few people can have experienced in these islands, and I never expect to have again.

At the end of the first half-hour, during which the good people of Killaloe must have thought a regiment was engaged in musketry drill, we were pulled up sharp by coming to a large drain of annoying dimensions, too deep to wade, and too wide to leap. After consideration, I tried the former operation, thereby filling my long boots with water—an unpleasant incident, which was repeated several times during the day. D— was not more fortunate. By one o'clock we had not more than half shot over the meadows, for progress was slow, owing to the difficulty of walking and the number of birds; but, to our dismay, we ran short of cartridges.

There was nothing for it but to return to the yacht and fill some more, and this we did, taking advantage of the opportunity to partake of some excellent stew concocted by our skipper.

Whilst we were filling cartridges—with, I fear, dangerous rapidity—a voice came down the hatchway that a duck was among the reeds, and that "I'll do my besht to take yer honour straight to him." I went on with my work, having, from sad experience, very little belief in reports of ducks in the reeds. D—, however, departed with our skipper in the dinghy, and in ten minutes, during which I heard two reports of his gun, returned with a splendid mallard—a heavy bird, thanks to the past few weeks of mild weather.

Ten minutes later we were again on the meadows, where the birds which we had missed in the morning seemed to have returned, for they were as plentiful as ever. All through the day I do not think there was an interval of ten minutes (luncheon time, of course, excepted) in which we were not putting up snipe. Before we had thoroughly worked the whole of our very happy hunting-ground it became too dark to see, and, though neither of us were first-rate snipe shots, we brought back to the yacht quite a load of the excellent little long-billed birds.

We did not see Mr. P— before we left Killaloe, to thank him for the capital day's shooting he had given us, but we afterwards heard that having never known the meadows hold many snipe, and hearing the frequent reports of our guns, he imagined we were simply slaughtering coots and water-hens, on which, as a rule, an Irishman deems powder and shot wasted.

There can be no doubt that the weather favoured us. The frost and snow came on very suddenly, and the direction of the wind was such that these meadows were in a particularly sheltered position. But such a combination of circumstances is not very unusual in winter, and there were probably some other reasons, maybe beyond human comprehension, which led to this extraordinary assemblage of snipe.

After dinner D—and I spent an hour, crouching in the snow, waiting for the evening flight of ducks. D— behind a hawthorn bush on the dam commenced by Brian Boru, and I among the trees which now crown the former stronghold of that mighty chieftain. Unfortunately there was no wind, and though we saw hundreds of ducks, all flew high above our heads and well out of range.

It was a cold, dreary vigil; the crescent moon shone dimly through the slight haze, and no sound broke the stillness of the windless night. The gloomy mountains seemed in the semi-darkness to tower up behind me to an enormous height. Suddenly, while I was watching, a beautiful transformation scene took place far up the lake, for there the clouds must have parted, and the moonbeams poured down on the glistening water, rocky islands, and rolling moorland, making a brilliant vignette. It was as if one were in a theatre in which the lights had been turned down, while on the stage a soft, moonlit scene was being presented.

Every now and again ducks and other wild fowl would pass high in the air above us, but, as I have said, they were much to distant too afford any chance of sport. Presently snow flakes began to fall gently and silently through the trees, and the silvery picture in the distance gradually faded away from my sight. I waited another ten minutes or so, then gave up the game as hopeless and returned with D— to the cosy cabin of the yacht.

It now and again happens in one's life that Sunday is somewhat inconveniently placed in the week, and this was a case in point. The following day we were burning to renew our attack on the snipe which had so opportunely taken possession of the water-meadows by the river. But it was the Day of Rest and we had perforce to leave them alone. It will be seen that the little birds took an extremely mean advantage of our consideration and simple piety.

While the men went to mass D— and I took the dinghy and explored the lake. In the evening the snipe seemed as plentiful as ever, wisps flying repeatedly over the water meadows and pitching here and there.

"An early start to-morrow," said I.

"I should just think so, me bhoy," said D—, and we hugged ourselves at the prospect of another great day with those birds.

Monday came, we turned out early, hurried over breakfast, and burning with eagerness were put on shore, gun in hand, and with enough cartridges to slay a hundred brace of snipe.

And the result of it all?

Devil a snipe could we find! If I may be pardoned an Irishism.

The frost held, the hills were snow-covered, and the wind was in the same quarter as before. Why had they gone, and whither? I doubt if anyone could answer these questions. They were there on Sunday, so our shooting on Saturday had not scared them. The only solution I can give to the problem is that, having invaded these meadows in such numbers, they speedily exhausted all available food, and therefore left in search of new feeding grounds.

A Gillaroo Day.

> " Come May, with all thy flowers,
>   Thy sweetly-scently thorn,
>   Thy cooling evening showers,
>   Thy fragrant breath at morn.
>   When May-flies haunt the willow
>   When May buds tempt the bee."
>
> MOORE.

> " Now's the day, and now's the hour !"
>   See the cloudy swarm doth lour !
>   Now, ye trout, arise and kill
>   And of plenty take your fill !
>   Ope your eyes and shake your fins !
>   Now the feast of feasts begins !
>   For the revels all prepare !
>   O the dainties rich and rare !"
>
> COTSWOLD ISYS.

CHAPTER VI.

A GILLAROO DAY.

From the quick-twisting, scaping snipe to the yellow-sided, large-spotted, thick-set gillaroo-trout is, in Ireland, but a step from the marshy lake side into the leaky lake boat. In early summer many a fish of the interesting variety mentioned might, for instance, be seen rising by anyone looking out over the lough from Brian Boru's old stronghold. It was curious that on some days the gillaroo seemed to feed more readily than the ordinary lake trout, while on others not one would be taken.

There was one smiling morn I remember, when the rippling water, gentle breeze, and a sun more or less veiled by light fleecy clouds made it a model fishing day. But what availed the day when, though it was the height of the green drake festivities, not a fly nor rise of fish was to be seen?

"We must have fish, Mick, for some people are coming to dinner to-night," said I.

"Faith, an' we will," said he; and we did.

A few minutes later my man's strong arms—it was all arm-work with Mick—were urging our trim little Athlone-built cot along a rocky but unfishful piece of shore, I in the meantime baiting a Chapman spinner attached to a well leaded trace, with a preserved bleak brought all the way from England. That having been done, a 3-inch silver phantom was quickly fastened to the end of a long and fine but strong trace rigged up on a second rod.

We were hurrying along at anything but a fishing speed, when the rod bearing the phantom, which I had laid down for a moment, was nearly pulled out of the boat, the reel whizzed round at a furious rate, and overran; a big silvery fish leaped high in the air, fell into the water, and—the pity of it—was gone, the hooks having been literally dragged out of its mouth. All my own fault, of course; but in the name of all the round towers in Ireland, who would expect to hook a salmon where never salmon in the memory of man was hooked before?

Well, it was no use crying over lost fish; so we went on our way towards a cluster of islands where trout and, in places, pike abounded. In the course of a quarter of an hour the line, which was in a horrid mess, was disentangled, and about that time we found ourselves at a fine patch of weeds a little distance out in the lake. Round these weeds, and so close that I caught in them every few minutes, Mick carefully and skilfully pulled the cot, and, before we had gone a dozen yards a considerable tug told me that a pike, which was in ambush, had seen my bleak, and, darting out to bite, been bitten. Immediately I struck, and the pike felt the prick or resistance of the hooks, he made for the weeds, and much ado I had to keep him out of them. Mick, who knew his business thoroughly, assisted me much by quickly rowing away from the pike's stronghold, and, thanks to sound tackle, the fish was turned, and in due course came up to the surface to gnash his teeth at us, after the manner of pike, and be gaffed. Eleven and a half pounds, and in excellent condition, if you please, though the summer had hardly begun. I need hardly say that pike were not preserved in the lake, but were killed at all times of the year.

Another scientific turn round Pike Hall producing nothing but weeds, Mick again turned the cot's nose towards the aforesaid islands, and on the way, told me the time-honoured story of the Irish boatman who, having assured a nervous English gentleman that he knew every rock in the lake, added triumphantly, as at that moment the boat had a hole knocked in her, "and, begor! there's one of them same."

"There's one of them, indeed," said I, for just as Mick finished his story, a fish which had probably been courteously waiting for the end of the tale, seized the somewhat damaged remains of my spirituous bleak, which, attached to the pike tackle, was trailing behind the boat. The fish was a game one, clearly no pike. Three times, after being reeled nearly up to the boat, did he dash away again, and, though the tackle was strong, I feared to put a very great strain on it, lest the hooks might break away. At last he showed himself, and Mick and I exclaimed almost together "A gillaroo!"

His short thick shape, large spots, and golden yellow sides betrayed his species—or should I not say variety? —at once. The thickened stomach could be easily felt. When landed he turned 3¾lb. on the steel-yard. This was good luck indeed, and we almost ceased to grieve for the salmon.

Having arrived at the islets, the pike rod was taken in, and the cot was rowed by rocky points and over shallows, all sure places for trout. In the place of the heavily leaded pike trace and Chapman spinner, I used the phantom minnow and a long unleaded trace, and let out at least fifty yards of line behind the boat. When trolling for trout in lakes, I have frequently proved the value of a long line—far longer than is generally used. The bait mentioned, a silver phantom, is first-rate for large lake trout and gillaroo. It was first shown me by an angler who has fished the Shannon for thirty-five years or more.

The phantom proved as attractive as usual, and before we had gone far, a trout of 1½lb. got hooked in a respectable manner, and was landed. Then we passed twice or thrice over a sunken island, and I am sorry to say that two less respectable trout pricked themselves badly, but managed to get away. Whether they were large or small fish I had no opportunity of judging, but Mick, as usual, declared they were the biggest fish of the season.

Leaving the sunken rocks, we passed on to a third island, round which the water was fairly deep along the shore. Mick now kept the boat close in to land. For some time nothing happened. On we went slowly and quietly—so quietly, indeed, that an otter which had its back turned to us, and was apparently eating a fish, took no notice whatever, though we passed within fifteen yards of it. Rounding a rocky point we came into a beautiful bay. Immense lichen-covered rocks—among which grew, somewhat fantastically, stunted ash trees and larch—lined its shores. In this bay a trout seized the phantom, but for some time I thought the fish was a pike, it played so heavily. As I brought it alongside the boat we saw it was another gillaroo, and it was caught in a very curious manner. One hook of the tail triangle was caught in its side, while the gut on which was tied the flying triangle at the head of the bait had gone round the nose of the fish, the triangle itself catching into the swivel at the head of the bait. Never was fish more hopelessly hooked. It weighed 2lb. 6oz.

The breeze had freshened considerably while we had been fishing, and, being in our favour, and the cot sailing well, we were wafted home to lunch in no time. The brace of gillaroos were made into cutlets and fried in butter. Right good they were—redder than salmon, curdy, flaky, and firm. Who, I wonder, was the ignoramus who informed Dr. Day that the gillaroo trout of Lough Derg were "soft, colourless, and inferior," for thus they are described in "British and Irish Salmonidæ," p. 194? I have caught some hundreds of these fish out of the Shannon, and certainly prefer them to salmon.

After lunch there was a small rise of Mayfly, and, Mick and I took a few drifts across the bay with dapping tackle. The first drift produced nothing, but during the second, when half-way across the bay, an enormous trout neatly picked the fly off my hook, and, rolling over as he did so, showed a broad golden side, which could hardly have belonged to a fish of less than 8lb. or 9lb. weight. That, too, I think, was a gillaroo, but could not speak with absolute certainty, for, though we drifted over the spot several times, he never rose again—at least, not to my fly.

Then the breeze shifted slightly, and, blowing from the west, freshened considerably. It was now a difficult matter to keep the fly on the dancing waves, but in the course of the hour which followed the rise of the big trout, I managed to pick up a brace of about 1½lb. each, neither of which had gillaroo markings; but, on being cleaned, the larger of the two was found to have the thickened stomach, which is the chief peculiarity of *Salmo stomachicus*.

We had come to the end of our last drift, and our friends had arrived, and we were being hailed to go in to dinner. The wind was blowing harder than ever, and Mick was shifting his seat to commence rowing. A moment later my fly, which was within a few yards of the rocks, would have been off the water. At that instant the line straightened a little, and, with faint hopes of the cause being a fish, I struck somewhat carelessly. It was a fish, and a good one.

Our position was peculiar, for the boat was drifting rapidly on to the rocks, on which the water was breaking; and between us and the rocks was the fish, which I vainly tried on my light tackle to lead towards and round the stern of the craft. But no; he would neither be led nor driven, and straight under the boat he went. Thanks to a Nottingham reel, and my rod being fitted with first-rate rings, I was able to give the trout unlimited line, which was clearly the only thing to be done under the circumstances. And meanwhile Mick quickly got out a scull and skilfully poled the boat off the dangerous shore. The line, by some great good fortune, slipped from under the cot without catching on the keel; and on reeling up, to our surprise we found the fish was still on, a fact of which, owing to the slack line, he himself was possibly in ignorance. He fought gamely, weighed just 4lb., and was a gillaroo. A few days later, by a really curious coincidence, I rose, hooked, and landed another fish, ¼lb. heavier, almost in the same spot. That fish also bolted under the boat.

"Gillaroo" is a word which certainly conveys no particular meaning to the general reader, though those who have perused the foregoing pages will have gathered that it is some kind of trout. Few questions in natural history have given rise to greater speculation than the number of species of trout, the relation of trout to salmon, and whether both trout and salmon were originally sea-fish or freshwater fish. As regards salmon, some hold the opinion that they, like the smelt, (which, it is interesting to note, is a member of the same family), is a sea-fish only visiting fresh water for spawning purposes. Others consider that it is a fresh water fish which finding insufficient sustenance in the river in which it is born, is forced to go to the sea in search of food, only returning for matrimonial reasons.

That there is a close relationship between sea-trout and the ordinary brown trout of our rivers is beyond question. In baby-hood they are practically indistinguishable, and even the young of the salmon bears a very close resemblance to the young of the brown trout and sea trout. Brown trout vary in appearance according to their age, sex, food, and surroundings, and it was formerly supposed a great many species existed; but the modern, and undoubtedly better opinion (founded on the careful observations of fish culturists who have different fish under their eyes from the egg state till they have attained a weight of five pounds or more), is that there is only one species of trout, or at least of the trout which always remain in fresh water. To give an instance, the ordinary observer on seeing a trout taken from Loch Leven would say it was a different kind of fish entirely to the trout taken from almost any other river or lake in the kingdom; but fish culturists who have reared Loch Leven trout in captivity find that when enclosed in ponds and fed on the same food as fish reared from the eggs of common burn trout, the characteristics common to the fish of Loch Leven are lost, and there is practically nothing to distinguish them from Salmo fario.

It is difficult to come to any definite conclusion concerning gillaroos. In the Shannon lakes they abound. The large ones—over 2½lb.—can nearly always be known by their shape and colour; but I have frequently taken smaller trout with no distinctive markings, which, however, had the gillaroo stomach. The ordinary trout of the lakes feed on very small fresh-water snail, but, with the exceptions referred to, have ordinary stomachs, and if the stomach should thicken under the influence of shell-fish in one case, why should it not in another? I am inclined to think, however, that the large gillaroos feed more extensively on snails than do the smaller gillaroos, or the ordinary brown trout, for the bellies of the larger gillaroos I examined were nearly always full of shellfish.

Two most interesting and important points relating to the causes of the gillaroo stomach are noted by the late Dr. Day. On the authority of Thompson, he states that the coats of other species of Salmones than S. Fario became muscular when shell-fish was the diet. Sir Humphrey Davy also observed that "the char of the lakes of Southern Austria, feeding similarly (to the gillaroo trout) have a like thick stomach."

A gillaroo said to have been reared by Mr. Capel from eggs brought from Lough Melvin, was examined and found to have the stomach of an ordinary brook trout; and Dr. Day also stated, though apparently not from personal observation, that the thickening diminishes or entirely disappears in gillaroo raised in new localities.

But, while the shell-fish diet seems to account for the

thickened stomach, and possibly also for the deep red flesh, does it also account for the very distinctive shape and markings of the Irish gillaroos? To a certain extent I think it does. As regards the large spots, the gillaroo simply seems to me to have the appearance of a lake trout in the most prime condition. The golden or yellow belly is common to most trout which haunt the more sheltered side of a lake where water-lilies, weeds, and other aquatic vegetation are usually found. The side which is rocky and sterile, owing to the storms which beat upon it, usually produces more silvery fish with steely blue shadings.

As to shape, the gillaroo is peculiar, in being exceedingly short and thick. This must also be in a measure owing to the plentiful supply of nourishing food which he absorbs, and also to his living in a lake, and, except at spawning time, not frequenting running water. Where torrents have to be stemmed Nature soon moulds her living crafts on more graceful lines.

The Fish That Did Not Fail.

"*If so be the angler catch no fish, yet he hath a wholesome walk to the brook side, pleasant shade, by the sweet silver streams; he hath good air, and sweet smells of fine fresh meadow flowers; he hears the melodious harmony of birds; he sees the swans, herns, ducks, waterhens, cootes, etc., and many other fowle with their brood, which he thinketh better than the noise of hounds, or blast of horns, and all the sport that they can make.*"

BURTON.

"*I have sometimes tried at a rising fish,*
With a faith that has seen him served on my dish;
In vain; while I've aimlessly dangled the line,
And hook'd with surprise a troutie fine.

Anon I have cast an aimless fly
With no hope at all, and have let it lie,
When it seem'd in the open jaws to fall
Of a fish that cared not to rise at all."

COTSWOLD ISYS.

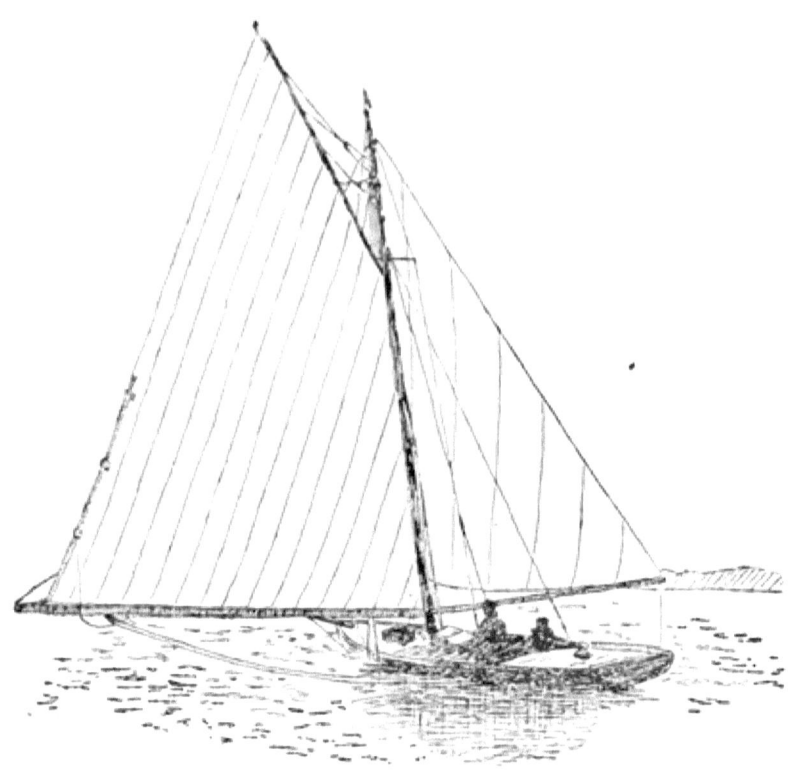

CHAPTER VII.

THE FISH THAT DID NOT FAIL.

An angler beyond all others has the privilege, established by long custom, of breaking off from the mere narration of contests with fish, to indulge in chatty moralisations and not too deep philosophic reflections more or less remotely connected with his subject. I deem no apology necessary, therefore, in leading up to two angling incidents which happened to me on Lough Derg, with a few remarks on the singularities of the creatures which those bloodthirsty humans who term themselves "gentle anglers" love to destroy.

In the first place I venture to assert that every angler will concur in the statement that fish, and those of Ireland not excepted, are perverse things at the best. On certain occasions they exhibit an obstinacy which would out-mule a mule. Who has not striven vainly to make up his third brace of trout? Five beautiful fish are lying in the creel, the rise has been a good one, and the difficulty of catching a sixth appears infinitesimal. Remarks on the subject of the dinner hour, of the dressing bell having rung, are treated by the angler of limited experience with contempt. Only half a minute, he demands, and he will have that trout. He really must make up his third brace. But the old hand, who knows better, sighs a sad sigh, or maybe smiles a cynical smile ; for long years have taught him that there is no trout in the world so difficult to catch as the trout required to make up the number on which the angler has set his heart. Sometimes it is roach, sometimes perch, or, maybe, jack. Up to a certain point the fish have fed madly, and that point arrives immediately we decide how many fish we mean to catch before we leave the water. The angler, therefore, should decide nothing, but take what fortune offers. Confidence is all important, but it must not be confidence in one's power to catch a certain number of fish, but simply the assured feeling that the fly or other tackle in use is just the right thing. Beyond that no man should go, those who are wise being careful to despond rather than hope. A good and vigorous grumble delivered at the weather before setting out is helpful. At the end of the day it is futile.

Your unsuccessful angler is invariably the man who sets out full of hope and with an empty basket, and returns in the evening with despair predominating, explanations profuse, and basket unchanged. The successful angler, on the other hand, bounds out in the morning determined to do his best, but quite prepared to catch nothing. Certainly the fish have every appearance of knowing this, and appear to appreciate this tribute to their acuteness by rising most freely to the man who least expects to catch them.

The perverseness and mule-like obstinacy to which I have referred are, as a rule, in evidence when a fish is particularly required for the table, or when a non-angling friend pays our country house a visit and we take him to the side of the stream to illustrate the delights of our favourite art, and how easy it is for a professor like ourselves to catch a trout.

Never by any chance does that friend see a trout in the landing net; unless, indeed, he himself takes the rod in his hand, with some such observation as "Of course, it is no use a duffer like me attempting to catch a fish, but I wish you would show me how to chuck out a fly."

And he does chuck out a fly, as awkwardly and badly as a man can. There will then, and not otherwise, most certainly be a perverse fish lying at the tail of that patch of weeds on the shallow, which, out of pure cussedness, takes our tyro-friend's fly and causes him for the rest of the afternoon to assume an offensive air of superiority. This lasts until, having been bitten with the sport, he buys a rod of his own, and sets methodically to work, hopeful and confident. That confidence breaks the spell, and soon he finds out something concerning the perverseness of trout.

Now and again there seem to be exceptions to the rule which I have been endeavouring to formulate, but they are so rare and so remarkable as to be well worthy a page and a red letter in the angler's note book. For instance, there was a day in June, when the sun shone out as only a June sun can shine, and the waters of the great lough were smooth as any piece of lookingglass, the yacht being beautifully reproduced in the natural mirror—when no clouds hovered round the summits of the lofty mountains which afforded us protection gainst the Atlantic gales—when all things, from an angler's point of view, were as hopeless and useless and wretched and detestable as things could be. There were these unfortunate conditions, added to an almost empty larder (no shops within eleven miles), when our look-out sighted a boat, and, by the aid of the binoculars we discovered that seven friends from the opposite shore were rowing in our direction.

The mere fact that we were in Ireland, that our visitors were reaching the end of a water journey of five miles, were sufficient reasons in themselves for us to come to the conclusion that something in the way of lunch would be required; and there was that empty larder staring us in the face; and, teeming with fish, that tantalising placid lake, in which it seemed useless to wet a line. How the wife suggested catching a trout or two, and how the angler derided the idea, need not be set down here; of course it ended in the weaker vessel entering his boat and rowing off, at the risk of being called a fool by the peasants round the bay, most of whom knew a thing or two about fishing.

As I recall the events of that day I can almost feel

the rays of the June sun striking down on my devoted head from above, and striking up from the glassy lake into my equally devoted face, and can see the perspiration pouring down the face of Andy, who rowed me round point after point trolling a colley bait, or, as we should call it in England, a stone loach.

Further and further we went from the yacht, and nearer and nearer came the boat-load of hungry visitors; and then, oh joy! just as we passed an outstanding spit of land there was such a screech from the reel, followed by a flash of silver fifty yards in the wake of the boat. Of course there was a bank of weeds near, into which the fish could have dived.

It was well I expected to catch nothing that morning; it was well I concluded the fish would go into those weeds. Owing solely, I honestly believe, to being in just that state of mind which neutralised the unfortunate fact that a fish was needed for the table, I got a grilse of 7lb., the only fish of the kind taken in the lake during the season, and brought him home in triumph, reaching the yacht as our friends were arriving. How different would it have been had I gone out perfectly certain of my power to secure a gillaroo, or a lake trout, or a pike, or a dish of perch for my visitors!

There is a very singular sequel to this story. Some three weeks later my wife and I, with a crew of one, set sail across the lake in a small cutter yacht, to enjoy the pleasures of a garden party given by those same friends who had lunched on my grilse. When we were in the middle of the lake the wind fell. Having no sweeps on board we were compelled to wait patiently about a mile and a half from the opposite shore until seven o'clock in the evening. Through the glasses we could see the cars drive up to the lodge and the guests walk on to the lawn which sloped down to the water's edge. We also saw them play tennis for a while, refresh themselves, and depart.

When it is a case of a lady having provided a new dress for the occasion, and having advised the journey to be made in a rowing boat, the unfortunate husband having, against her opinion, insisted on a craft with sails, the position may perhaps be understood without any elaborate explanation. However, there did come a time in the evening when we reached the opposite shore; and I quietly chuckled to myself when I heard our hostess whisper to her husband something to the effect that there was no fish in the house, and indeed very little for dinner, so he must take the boat and go out with his man, Malone, and get a trout or two. He said that could "easily" be done—a fatal remark so far as he was concerned.

Being usually glad of an excuse to go fishing, I begged to join in the search after trout, and Mr. C— lent me one of his boats. Leaving my friend to fish round a little bay, I voyaged off with my man to the opposite point, where I had often seen large trout rising. I was most careful to expect nothing; in fact, I assured Andy, who was rowing me, that it was a practical impossibility that we should catch anything, but we would just try. Andy opined that we should "do our besht, and what could a man do more?"

It took us some twenty minutes to make the point, and by that time a slight favouring ripple, which might have helped us to a fish, had died away. Dark clouds were gathering, and just as we reached our fishing ground I heard distant thunder rumbling among the mountains. Then happened one of the strangest things I have ever seen in my life as a fisherman. A few fine spots of rain began to fall, and with them came down swarms of small black flies. Hardly had these touched the water, before, all around us, enormous trout began to show themselves and swim about with their back fins out of water, literally skimming the surface of the black flies which were powdering it.

When I first saw this remarkable exhibition of monsters, I certainly thought I should quickly catch a fine trout. So long as that was my state of mind not a fish would look at my flies which, it must be admitted, were a trifle large for use in calm water. But as hope departed, and I began to realise that I was doomed to failure that evening, so apparently did my chances increase.

When I had absolutely given up all hope, a fish, doubtless feeling that my despondency merited some reward, rose to one of my flies, and gave me as fine a piece of sport as any I had experienced in that lake. Before he was in the landing net the extraordinary rise of large trout was over.

I never before had any idea of the vast numbers of fish there must be in these big Irish waters. I should say that around me were not less than a hundred trout, and that none of them were under 3lb., and that many weighed as much as 8lb. or 9lb. The one I caught was beautiful, with silvery scales, and had perhaps paid the sea a visit at some time or another—who can say? He weighed about 6lb. During dinner—the trout proved firm and curdy as a fresh run salmon—I demonstrated to my host, who had caught nothing, the folly of his setting out to fish in a confident state of mind, and the good results to be obtained from a condition of piscatorial hopelessness.

* * * * *

There was no wind by which we could sail back that evening, but we borrowed a small boat and pleasantly crossed the lake by moonlight. During the row I remarked how wisely Providence shaped things, and that, had we not missed the garden party, I should not have caught my largest trout of the season. But the lady, who would have preferred the garden party, expressed dissatisfaction with Providence on that particular occasion.

Winter Sports of the Lake Dwellers.

*"Soon were heard on board the shouts and songs of the sailors
Heaving the windlass round, and hoisting the ponderous anchor,
Then the yards were braced, and all sail set to the west-wind
Blowing steady and strong."*

THE COURTSHIP OF MILES STANDISH.

*"He comes—he comes—the Frost
Spirit comes! and the quiet lake shall feel
The torpid touch of his glazing breath,
And ring to the skater's heel."*

J. GREENLEAF WHITTIER.

CHAPTER VIII.

WINTER SPORTS OF THE LAKE DWELLERS.

I NEVER yet was able to induce any one to believe that yachting, when the thermometer registers eight or nine degrees of frost, could be anything but unpleasant:

> When icicles hang by the wall,
> And Dick the shepherd blows his nail,
> And Tom bears logs into the hall,
> And milk comes frozen home in pail.

At such times life on the water is usually deemed a most undesirable existence ; but with plenty of clothing, exercise, sport, food, and one or two cheerful companions, it may be really very enjoyable, and of this I will venture an additional illustration to that given in Chapter V.

One winter's morning when the yacht was peacefully resting at her moorings in Youghal Bay (of course, not the Youghal of the east coast), our skipper, Sinbad, reported, ere we had left our berths, that the frost held, a dense mist o'erhung the lake, and that wildfowl were calling all round us.

"Get up, yer honours," he said ; "there's divil a duck this morning that wouldn't let you within ten yards of it."

Of course—D—and I tumbled out at once, and half-an-hour later were being sculled across the bay by Jim, who had thoughtfully "muffled" the oars to prevent the merry rattle of the row-locks advising the birds that their dread enemies were approaching.

We found the bay to be full of duck, divers, and coots, the latter, as usual, predominating. The fog was extraordinarily thick. Thirty yards from the boat we could distinguish nothing, and when the birds were only fifteen or twenty yards off, could not see them sufficiently distinctly to tell whether they were mallard, merganser, or teal. An hour's sculling about only resulted in the death of two coots which we had mistaken for duck, but the general chorus of "quacks" around us when we fired, showed that we had put up large flocks of more desirable wildfowl.

We had a compass with us, but our crew, unversed in its mysteries, soon became exceedingly nervous at being so far out in the lough, and land invisible. It was, therefore, no doubt, rather more on his own account than ours, that he begged us to make for the shore, where, so he said, we should be sure to find plenty of wildfowl on the rocks. However, we determined to devote another half-hour to the lough, and opportunities of shooting ducks we had without number, but it always happened that as soon as we sighted the birds they sighted us, and either dived or flew off while we were considering as to their variety. This is the sort of thing that happened about every ten minutes:

"Whist! there's a bird; there to yer honour's left!" would whisper Hall; and just as I was raising my gun to my shoulder would stop me with, "Arrah! don't shoot now, it's only a coot"—said in a loud voice. Then the supposed coot would, of course, fly off with a "quack! quack!" followed by a charge of shot sent uselessly after him through the mist; Jim exclaiming:

"Oh, begor, it was a duck afther all!"

Most tantalising work truly, and before the half-hour was up we made for the opposite shore, which, with the aid of my compass, was reached in about twenty minutes. On the way I winged a mallard which flew across the course of the boat, but, falling into the water, dived, came up out of sight, and was lost, so far as we were concerned, in the fog.

We found the shore fringed with ice, too thick to break through, yet not strong enough to bear us. After a time we effected a landing on an exposed point where the break of a very slight swell coming in from the lake had kept the ice from forming. There having been such numbers of birds in the open water, I was not very sanguine of finding many along the shore, but Jim declared they would be there in scores, and Jim was a native of the place, so, of course, would know better than his Saxon employers. What we did find was a few wary ducks perched on the extreme edge of the ice, and well out of range.

The ingenious Jim now proposed that he should row along by the shore, and cause the birds to fly over our heads. Waterfowl very rarely do anything of the kind under such circumstances, generally making for the open lake when disturbed. However, we were not sorry to be without our sagacious follower, so sent him off in the boat. D—and I then strolled round the bay, killing a few plover and a brace of snipe, which latter, frozen out everywhere else, had come down to a spring near the lough. That winter was a terrible one for the poor birds, and none suffered more than the long beaks. Curlew in particular died by hundreds, as their bleached skeletons, dotted here and there about the bogs in the following spring, testified.

About three o'clock we found ourselves at the other side of the bay, near where the *Tallyhassie* lay moored. For the past half-hour we had heard peals of laughter, by no means conducive to wild fowl-shooting, echoing over the water, and on a broad shallow, sheltered by a reed-bed, we came upon a merry party of our Irish friends thoroughly enjoying the first day's skating of the season. Our skates were on board the *Tally*, and, as only an hour of daylight remained, it was too late to fetch them; but, hearing that the best skating in the neighbourhood was to be obtained in Dromineer Bay, some two or three miles distant by water, we arranged a water and skating picnic for the following day, much to the delight of the younger members of the party.

In no corner of Great Britain have I had better or more varied sport than near those reed-beds by which my friends were skating that afternoon. On the broad shallows during the summer roam shoals of aldermanic rudd, always ready to take a fly of any kind or description, of which I will say more anon. Then there are the pike, little and big, which, especially in the spring, have their lairs among the reeds, attracted thither possibly by the hundreds of succulent flappers and other young wildfowl which abound. Duck are always there, and sometimes in great numbers, while in the deeper water, not a dozen yards away, I have made some capital bags of perch. Trout are there also, but not in great plenty, and occasionally, but this rarely, a salmon is to be found near the reeds. "It's a darlin' spot," as Paddy would say.

Arrived at the yacht, we were somewhat disturbed in mind on learning from Sinbad that Jim had not yet come back, for Jim could not swim. Our orders to him had been to row slowly round the bay, and if he had done this he must have reached the *Tallyhassie* some hours before us. He might have rowed into the sharp ice and stove a hole in the boat; or have attempted to cross the bay, in which case he would most certainly have gone astray, for without compass or some sound coming from the shore, or a slight breeze, the direction of which can be used as a guide, to row a boat straight in a fog is almost an impossibility. However, after we had fired guns and gone out on to the lake in our second boat blowing a foghorn at intervals, the rascal did turn up, some two hours or so after sundown, and declared he had been rowing round "just as we'd tould him intoirely."

We heard afterwards that he had spent a pleasant afternoon with some friends in a not far distant cottage.

Fair-weather summer-sailors can hardly imagine the luxury of a yacht's cabin in winter. How cosy it was that evening! Outside was the biting frost, rendered doubly intense by the chilly mist; the snow-covered, ghostlike larch-woods, and the cold dull lake. But inside—what a contrast! Steaming whisky-toddy, briar-root pipes doing duty right manfully, and cheery conversation, further enlivened by a song from our crew, who had an uncommon voice for a sailor, a sweet tenor—a song about going miles away across the ocean wide and then returning to Mary. What pleasant evenings they were, to be sure!—and pleasant days, too, though we did sometimes find ourselves frozen to the floor-boards of our leaky fishing-boat, while crouching down during the anxious operation of sailing up to flocks of wildfowl.

*   *   *   *   *

The following day was as great a contrast to its predecessor as was the cosy appearance of our cabin that evening to the bleak prospect outside.

> Full many a glorious morning have I seen
> Flatter the mountain tops with sovereign eye,

but none *more* glorious. A first-rate sailing breeze ruffled the surface of the lough, sweeping away all traces of the mist, and causing just the slightest possible swell to come rolling into Youghal Bay. Not a cloud marred the purity of the pale blue ether, and the sun did its best to shine, excelling in that respect all its previous winter performances. The snow on the larch-trees glistened in the sunshine, and all nature seemed bright and cheerful.

After breakfast there was a great stowing-away of spoon-baits and phantoms, between the triangles of which and ladies' dresses we had previously noticed a strange affinity. About ten o'clock our skating picnic party came on board, and, everything being in readiness, the mooring bridle was cast off, and away we sped over the blue water. A stiff breeze was blowing right into the bay, so we had to beat out, clearing Rinskaheen Point on the third tack. As we passed the point a veteran angler, grandsire to the youngsters on board, told me some stirring tales of the salmon which used to be killed in Lough Derg, Rinskaheen being in former times a very favourite stand for fly-fishermen. Both large trout and monster pike still frequent the shoal of rocks which run out for some distance, but it is several years since a salmon was caught there.

There are salmon in the lough, for they must pass through it to get to the fisheries of Meelick, Banagher, and Athlone; but, as was stated at a Fishery Inquiry held at Limerick, not above ten fish were killed on the whole lake during the previous season, and Lough Derg is over twenty miles long! I could tell how, when rowing past the point one summer's evening with a phantom minnow trailing some forty yards or so behind the boat, a salmon seized the bait, and out went twenty more yards of line in the twinkling of an eye. The reel unfortunately, overran, and the hooks came away. A fair angler—an angler of the fair sex, of course—unaccustomed to the peculiarities of wooden reels, was holding the rod at the time.

Why are salmon so scarce in the lake? For two reasons: the tidal waters are overnetted, and the spawning-grounds of the fish—the brooks and tributary rivers—are absolutely unprotected. Probably enough fish would reach the upper waters for breeding purposes if they were not poached; but if they were less netted, more fish passing up, a surplus would be left for the poachers. Overnetting, *plus* the poaching of spawning fish, means certain destruction to any fishery. It is only immediately above Limerick, in the Castle Connell and Killaloe waters, that any decent fishing is to be had in what ought to be the finest salmon river in the whole kingdom.

Asking pardon for this digression, I return to the ould *Tally*, which, passing Rinskaheen and Hazel Points with the wind on her beam, has a clear run into Dromineer Bay. We are no sooner in the bay than we see that on the sheltered side, near the mouth of the Nenagh river, a good many people are skating.

The youngsters get impatient. "Why not anchor at once? Why go right over the other side of the bay?" But we cannot yield to their entreaties, for storms rise with inconceivable rapidity on Lough Derg, and woe betide the unlucky yacht exposed to their full force! Sinbad knows every inch of the bay, and pilots us into a sheltered corner. Down comes the foresail, the *Tally* runs up into the wind, and the anchor plunges through fourteen feet of peat-stained water into good holding ground.

The dinghy is soon loaded—a little deeper, perhaps, than is altogether wise—and away go more than half our party to the opposite shore. Within half-an-hour all have been landed, and are gliding swiftly over a capital bit of ice some two or three acres in extent.

Grandpapa is the one exception. He pays a visit to an old crony, with whom he, doubtless, recalls many of the fishing, shooting, and skating incidents of half a century or more.

"We never have such winters as in my young days," says the old gentleman; "was it in '30 or '31 that the lake was frozen right across, and we skated to Portumna and back? There is no such skating nowadays; your eights and grapevines are not to be compared with a glorious run over fifteen or twenty miles of ice."

And some of us agree with him.

The praises of Irish girls have been sung so often that I will not repeat them; suffice it to say that, thanks to the charming sprightliness of Erin's daughters, social gatherings in Ireland, be they for dancing, tennis, or skating, are just twice as lively as similar affairs in England. I doubt if I ever enjoyed skating more than those few hours in Dromineer Bay. The society was all that could be desired, the surroundings picturesque. Near the mouth of the river was an old castle, behind which rose heather-covered hills, now clad in a white garb of snow. Looking to the westward, over some six miles of water, we could distinguish the precipitous mountains which, commencing at one side of Scariff Bay, trend away to Killaloe. The shore near which we were skating was prettily wooded, the snow on the trees glistening in the sunshine. Altogether it was very delightful.

About three o'clock Sinbad came ashore with a big kettle full of tea (already mixed, to save trouble), sundry viands, and several rugs, &c., for seats. To these (barring the rugs) we soon did full justice, for there is no lack of appetite about a skating picnic— quite the contrary. Tea over, we had yet another half-hour's skating before making sail for Youghal.

People read character in handwriting; did any one ever make such an attempt with skating? I fancy there is a good deal to be done in that way. See the youth, darting hither and thither over thick and thin ice, merrily laughing at each fresh mishap. Is he not reckless, daring, careless, and good-natured? Then the figure-skater who for two long hours persistently endeavours to cut a double three: he must possess a character remarkable for determination and perseverance, and yet, perhaps, a man who will waste those excellent qualities over trifles, if I may be pardoned for even hinting that a double three is a trifle. Rather let us say that our friend is a man who wishes to do everything he attempts well. Then watch that couple who have been gliding slowly, locked hand-in-hand ever since ten o'clock—and it is now three! Röntgen rays are not required to illuminate the condition of the hearts where Cupid holds sway. But enough of this: let others follow out the interesting theme.

* * * * *

The half-hour is up, all are aboard, and we beat slowly out of Dromineer Bay, for the wind has decreased. The ladies crowd into the cabin, and we of the sterner sex, leaving the deck to our skipper and his crew, follow as in duty bound. After a while someone remarks that singing sounds sweetly upon the water, and the suggestion being unanimously approved, is acted upon.

Before we have rounded the point the sun has set, and on deck it is intensely cold. Cocoa and tea are served out for the second time, Sinbad and Jim not being forgotten: for plenty of good food is as necessary to keep one warm as abundance of clothing: whiskey won't do it—a fact the truth of which I have never known an Irishman admit. In chatting and singing the time passes so quickly that the rattle of the foresail coming down somewhat astonishes us. Sinbad now informs us it is so dark he cannot see the mooring buoy, so we tell him to anchor the yacht. We lie to for a while, for our friends to be taken on shore, and an hour later we join them, finishing the night with an improvised dance.

Some may observe that on the whole yachting in winter weather may be made pleasant enough. The keen sportsman, on the other hand, may stigmatise the foregoing as feather-bed proceedings, and wax scornful. Possibly the estimation in which he holds the charterers of the *Tallyhassie* may rise a little if in subsequent pages I relate certain semi-arctic experiences which, while being less pleasant that those contained in the present chapter. appeal more strongly to the hardy sportsman.

Slob Trout.

*"Just there, where the water dark and cool
Lingers a moment in yonder pool,
   The dainty trout are at play;
And now and then one leaps in sight,
With sides aglow in the golden light
   Of the long, sweet summer day."*

CARL WARING.

CHAPTER IX.

SLOB TROUT.

On the wind-swept moorlands which lie between Mal Bay and the river Fergus rise a number of small streams. Some of these, mere brooks, flow westward, swell into salmon rivers in the course of a few miles, and after no great wanderings empty their amber-coloured waters into the Atlantic. Others are of a different watershed, and take a southerly direction. Two of these southern flowing streams unite near a Catholic place of worship, known among the peasants as the "Mountainy Chapel." Thus wedded, they jointly flow for about three miles through a romantic valley, tumble headlong from a ledge of rock into a pool some 30ft beneath, and, after boiling and surging considerably, bound along down rapids to an ancient bridge, below which, under the shadows of spreading ash trees, they calm down. Then away they hie to other rapids and larger pools, until finally, after flowing through a bridge of five low arches, they mingle with the brackish waters of the Shannon estuary.

In the three miles of river below the waterfall above mentioned the brown trout run very small, but after every flood fat, well-fed silver-sided fish come up from the Shannon, and (except when on spawning intent) stay in the fresh water a few days, only so long, probably, as the extra food brought down by the flood remains unexhausted. When nothing but the scant supply common to rocky streams is left, these fish of the estuary, wise in their generation, return to their slob (mud) banks, and there continue to grow and wax fat.

To the naturalist, who commonly styles him *Salmo estuarius*, this fish is a most interesting variety. To the local angler, who speaks of him as a "slob trout," he is almost as sport-giving as his first cousin of the sea. Most probably he is nothing more nor less than the ordinary brown trout, which, in its search after food, has found its way into brackish water; and that brown trout will so descend rivers is a strong argument in favour of the theory that sea trout are simply brown trout which have acquired migratory habits, or that brown trout are sea trout which have made their home in fresh water. In Day's "British and Irish Salmonidæ" (p. 146) are the following remarks on this fish, but the name by which he is known to the anglers of Clare and co. Limerick is not mentioned:

"By almost imperceptible degrees we find them (anadromous sea trout) in every country passing from one form into the other, which raises the question of which form Salmo orcadensis, Salmo estuarius, etc., most resemble, the anadromous Salmo trutta or the freshwater Salmo fario. Believing the two latter to be

merely the extreme limits of one species, it becomes unnecessary to decide whether the diminution in the number of the vomerine teeth is symptomatic of the fresh-water form developing towards its larger relative the anadromous sea trout, or whether it is the sea trout retrograding towards its par dentition, or that which is often, but by no means always, persistent in Salmo fario. Colours, it is true, are not very reliable, but these forms more nearly approach the fresh-water than the saline varieties, a change which appears invariably to occur sooner or later in anadromous forms which become permanent residents in fresh water."

This fish of the estuary was, I believe, first mentioned by Dr. Knox in 1835, who pronounced it a new species. He obtained it at the mouth of the Nith, and also recorded it from the Kyle of Bute, Loch Fyne, the Forth, and the Esk in Yorkshire. Mr. Ogilby ("Royal Dublin Society," 1885, p. 527) mentioned the large estuary trout found about Portrush, and known locally as "dolochan." They appeared to be large brook trout, splendidly spotted and coloured, but without any silvery appearance.

"These fish," wrote Mr. Ogilby, "though living so long" (query, how long?) "in salt or brackish water, never assume a silvery appearance; in fact, some of the most brilliantly coloured and spotted trout I have ever seen were taken in almost pure salt water, close to the mouth of the Bann."

I mention Mr. Ogilby's experience with these Portrush

fish because the most noticeable characteristic of the trout
I caught in the river I have mentioned was their silvery
sides. At Galway estuarine trout are not uncommon.
Specimens were sent to Dr. Günther, who christened the
variety *Salmo gallivensis*.

* * * * *

It had rained for two days and two nights as only it
can rain in Ireland and Scotland. Tiny streamlets were
good-sized rivers, and rivers had become raging, foaming
torrents. One morning at breakfast, the deluge having
abated, my host said I could not do better than take the
car to the waterfall about midday, by which time the
river would have fallen a good deal, and though it would
not be by any means in good order, still there was the
chance of a brace or two of slob trout, particularly if I
took some worms. The worms I left behind, not loving
those baits for trout in muddy water, killing though
they are; the rest of the advice I followed, and about
one o'clock found myself standing by the side of a ruined
mill, looking down on the mimic maelstrom below the
fall.

Ireland is a country of ruins, the result perhaps of a
too copious supply of building material, combined, of
course, with poverty, emigration, and desertion. Irishmen
build their houses as birds build their nests, and in some
instances forsake them as readily. Stones are to be had
for the picking up; mud to place between the stones
there is in abundance, and the rushes, which make excellent thatch, grow freely in the bogs. As for timber, even

"TINY STREAMLETS WERE GOOD-SIZED RIVERS."

if his honour will not allow a few larch trees to be felled, why sure the bogwood will do. And so a house, such as it is, is run up in a few weeks, and when, after years, the roof lets in too much water, and the ground around has grown foul, it is no great matter to run up another dwelling fifty yards distant, which, as you may observe, is not intimately connected with the subject of slob trout. But when the water is in anything but good order one is in no great anxiety to begin, and the sight of ruined cottages on the way to the river—to say nothing of a ruined castle, two ruined churches, and one ruined mill—caused some such thoughts as I have jotted down to run through my head.

One thing was clear—clearer than the water by far—I was not to catch many fish that day. During the night there had evidently been a great flood. The grass on the banks had been washed flat, and leaves, sticks, and other *débris* of storm were scattered about, four feet at least above the present level of the water. Even now the river was eighteen inches or more above summer level, and a great tearing, roaring, coffee-coloured torrent dashed through the rapids below the waterfall pool. Not wetting a fly here, I climbed up a steep bank, and, making my way by the priest's house and across the glebe lands, soon reached an old stone bridge, above and below which were two fine pools. From the bridge looking up stream was a charming pastoral scene, which I made a mental note to photograph at the first opportunity. The pools I fished carefully, but rose nothing except small brown **trout of** the size too commonly found in salmon **rivers. Some five or six of** these were whisked **on shore, and then I sought to** make **my way** lower down **the river.**

The cattle in those **parts must be** wonderful climbers, if the barricades which divide **the** fields **are** really **necessary. Imagine, first of all,** a ditch ; **then a stone wall,** covered with sods ; on the other **side a fine growth of thorn bushes,** and **over all** brambles **innumerable. I commend this arrangement to the attention of the War Office. It is almost impregnable. Years** before, among those same brambles or **their predecessors,** a lovely new mackintosh **had been rent to** smithereens. Wiser now, the angler **threw** his mackintosh over **the barricade, and essayed to follow.** Five different places **he tried, five times** he **failed, and** then, **to the** great amusement of **two gossoons who were sitting on the hill-top,** found **himself obliged to make a detour of a quarter of a mile, which incidentally** necessitated the **crossing of** several similar **but less** impregnable erections. **Never, I** believe, since **fly was first cast, was there such a** thorny **path down a river's** bank.

Regaining **the river, I** found myself by **a** long deep **pool, into** which **the water gently** glided, **the bottom** of **which was, I afterwards discovered, of gravel. Several careful casts at the head of the pool** produced nothing, **but** half-way towards the tail, **right under** my own **bank, a** trout of about half **a** pound seized a dropper, **dashed** out into the current, **and** across **to** the opposite

"A CHARMING PASTORAL SCENE."

bank immediately under some blackberry bushes, with which the line instantly became marvellously intertwisted. The bad fifteen minutes which supervened can be easily imagined by any one who has had a line similarly circumstanced. As quickly as one foot of the line was disentangled, two feet got caught up somewhere else. How that line was ever released I can hardly say. Perhaps I manœuvered after the manner of the Irish schoolboy, who was late for school. "For every step I took forward I slipped two back, sir," said he.

"Then how did you come at all?" queried the schoolmaster, cane in hand.

"Begor, I just walked the other way," was the ready reply.

Whatever the manner of doing it, the line was freed and, best of all, the trout was still at the end of it, but not a slob trout, only a rather ill-conditioned brown thing, which may have been washed down over the waterfall above where brownies were very plentiful. Nothing more rose in the pool, and coming to a creek and a series of ditches, blackthorn hedges, and brambles innumerable, I thought the best thing to do was to get back up-stream, cross the stone bridge, and fish down the other side of the river. This having been done, not without much groaning and lamentation, and a half hour more or less wasted, I came round to the other side of the long pool, wherein the half-pounder had risen. Here there seemed no need to pause, but taking one or two careless casts as I walked along, a fish rose to my tail-fly just as it passed the centre of the stream. My cast was rather finer than was necessary for water of that colour, so the trout had to be dealt with somewhat tenderly.

After a couple of minutes' play the fish came close to the bank, but unpleasantly near the tail of the pool, where the stream was strong. Carefully I sunk the landing-net behind him, and sought to let him drop down into it; but, seeing me, he dashed from the bank, and was instantly carried away into the rapids. Fortunately, the bank was clear for some little distance, and after a smart run of fifty yards, during which the gut ought to have been broken fifty times, I brought up the fish in a small eddy behind a good-sized rock. He seemed pretty well played out, but before I could get the net under him sheered out into the stream, which carried him away once more. Another run, and then before me rose an Irish barricade of the kind already described, and a little lower the river leaped down a rocky gorge, where fish might live, but no man. Then luck favoured me; for a few yards the water on my side of the river eddied, and, seeing my chance, I guided the half-drowned fish towards the bank, held him for an instant, and netted him.

There he lay, my first slob trout, and very pretty he looked; back rather brown, but sides brilliantly silvered, bearing good-sized dark spots and a very few red ones. When releasing the fly, I noticed something peculiar in the fish's mouth. On careful examination I came to the conclusion that it was the partially digested remains of a shrew mouse which had been carried away by the flood.

Then followed another scramble, and a considerable detour, and half sliding, half walking down a bank I came suddenly upon a long, deep pool where salmon might well have been. Except for those aforesaid falls, the river would, doubtless, have contained salmon; but, in reply to certain suggestions as to blasting and salmon ladders, the very pertinent remark was made that the salmon, which would ruin the excellent brown trout fishing, now obtainable above the waterfall, would all be caught in the spawning season by peasants on the moor. So perhaps things were better as they were, though slob trout, like sea trout, might have done very well side by side with the larger fish.

The river was too much coloured and high for successful fishing in the long, deep pool, and I hardly tried it; but on other occasions when I visited it I was fairly successful. One day, indeed, it seemed full of fish, every cast producing a rise; but the stream through the pool was hardly perceptible, and there was no wind to ruffle the surface. This caused the fish to rise very short, so that I caught few. Irish flies are very often tied with rather long tails, and on some days the fish rise just so short as to touch the tail of the fly and miss the hook. Pluck after pluck is felt, but nothing is landed. Behind every stone in the pool there seemed to be two or three trout lurking, and many of these would follow the fly, making several darts at it but rarely summoning up enough courage to take it in their mouths.

Taking out a pair of scissors I trimmed the fly I was using down to the most meagre dimensions, and then began to catch a few fish. It was certainly the best holding pool in that part of the river, and one day in springtime the two sons of the owner of the water made an immense bag of fish, using worms as bait. But this was in their boy-hood when they had not fully felt the fascination and claims of the fly-rod.

Leaving the long pool I again crossed the river and rose a fish of about a pound on the edge of a shallow pool. A second cast produced no result; so, as the water had fined down somewhat, I tried a smaller fly. To this he rose, but came short, and as an experiment a Derbyshire bumble was put up. This seemed to suit his slobship, and a few minutes later his silvery form graced my basket. Lower down the river the small brown trout were rising freely, but I took no more slob trout that afternoon.

Later on in the week, when the water was in better order, the fishing for these estuarine trout improved, and I was much more successful, catching some in the tidal portions of the river, as well as higher up. This was late in the summer, when the fish were neither in the best condition nor in the most taking humour. Early spring fishing is the best, for these slob trout recover their condition in the estuary very quickly after spawning. In a letter from an Irish friend, dated

THE SLOB-TROUT RIVER.

January 7, I read: "If I can before Saturday shake off a cold which I have caught in some mysterious way, I think I shall try for slob trout in the tidal part of the river. They have been caught there in prime condition at the beginning of February, and very likely I shall find them good even now."

The variations in the spawning season in different rivers is very singular, and I have found no reason to account for it. Trout are not often fished for in September, but in some rivers they do not spawn until January. In this slob trout stream, however, it is evident they must have deposited their eggs early in the autumn to be in order by February, though they certainly appear to regain their condition more quickly than would trout which habitually remain in fresh water. This is no doubt owing to the bountiful feeding which they get in the estuary, whence probably they descend after spawning is over.

Icebound, and a Wild=goose Chase.

> "*The ice was here, the ice was there,
> The ice was all around.*"
>
> THE RIME OF THE ANCIENT MARINER.

> "*Freeze, freeze, thou bitter sky,
> Thou doth not bite so nigh
>   As benefits forgot;
> Though thou the waters warp,
> Thy sting is not so sharp
>   As friend remember'd not.*
>
> *Heigh, ho! sing heigh, ho! unto the green holly;
> Most friendship is feigning, most loving mere folly;
>   Then heigh, ho, the holly!
>   This life is most jolly.*"
>
> AS YOU LIKE IT.

CHAPTER X.

ICEBOUND, AND A WILD-GOOSE CHASE.

I HAVE mentioned that Lough Derg possesses tributary streams which in winter afforded us pike when the fish of the lake seemed quite off the feed, or had retreated to some unapproachable winter fastnesses. One of these was a small river rising among the mountains some distance above Scarriff. It flowed past the little white-washed, slate-roofed town of that name into Scarriff Bay, a long, narrow arm of the Lough.

On pike intent and with a fair wind, we set sail one winter's afternoon for the bay and arrived there an hour or so before nightfall. The river being fairly deep, we were able to sail up it a short distance, and anchor the *Tallyhassie* about a hundred yards within its mouth.

On one side of the bay are the rugged range of mountains which trend to Killaloe, on the other a series of reed-beds bordering flat meadow lands. A quarter of a mile from the mouth of the river are two small islands which stand sentry-like in the bay, and narrowing it at this point afford very fair shelter for yachts unless the wind blows straight in. Looking up the lake we could see on Holy Island an elevated round tower, one of the finest specimens of its kind remaining. Under its shadow are the ruins of an old monastic establishment and a little graveyard, which is still used. To be buried there is considered by the superstitious peasantry a long step towards eternal happiness, and at the time we were cruising about the lake there was a man living on its shores, who having had a limb taken off in an operation had it buried on Holy Island in advance of his body, "for," said he, "what would I do in Paradise wid only one arm?"

The island, with which we were fated to become better acquainted the following day, is of no great extent, but the soil, enriched by the interments of centuries, grows a grass which fattens cattle with such rapidity that the farmers willingly give as high rent for it as for any grazing land in Ireland. In the spring time the white narcissus blooms freely all over it, and here and there one comes upon clumps of golden daffodils. Whether in consequence of its profitable pasture, lovely spring flowers, ancient monuments, or passport to Paradise, I cannot say, but for some reason or another the peasants have made up their minds that it is inhabited by the "good people," as they term the fairies.

There are, or are known to have been, about a hundred round towers in Ireland, of which seventeen or eighteen are almost perfect. As to their origin and uses archæologists are absolutely ignorant, and as a consequence have discussed the subject *ad nauseam* without advancing a single step our knowledge of these mysterious remains of ages long past. They were watch towers said one, gnomons for making astronomical observations said another, an emblem of thallic worship said a third. Here are human bones said a fourth, therefore they are sepulchral monuments. "Nonsense; all nonsense," declares in effect a more modern savant. "Is not the Irish for Round Tower *Cuilceach*, which also means a reed—the reed shaken by the wind—John the Baptist. Believe me, they were used as baptisteries."

The Round Tower on Holy Island is similar to but more lofty than the one at Clonmacnoise illustrated on page 9.44. It lacks the conical roof required to make it a complete structure of the kind. Round about it are the remains of a number of chapels or churches which reminded me of the tower and seven churches at Clonmacnoise, where it may be remembered we gave Mick Flanigan boiled coot for lunch.

* * * * *

But let us return to the auld *Tally*. Leaving D. to superintend the preparation of our evening repast, for neither of our men had great knowledge of the culinary art, I set off for an hour's row round the bay, taking my gun with me. The wind had died away, but the air seemed to have become suddenly much colder. Up to this time there had been no frost, but pushing my boat through some reeds I heard a crackling against the bows, and found that around the water line of each reed was gathering a little sparkling collar of ice. The sun was setting, and as it went down it left a dark lurid glow behind it such as is

K *

only seen in the coldest weather. A strange silence had suddenly come over the land. The wild birds were hushed, and though flocks of curlew and plover were making their way to their feeding grounds, they uttered not a note. A hard and lasting frost had set in, and they knew it, and were possibly terrified by their knowledge.

Finding no ducks, I poled my boat through the reeds to the lapwings' and curlews' line of flight, and then patiently waited. Many birds flew over my head, but all out of shot. The red slowly left the sky, and the cold getting more intense, I determined to seek the yacht. But I was not to go home empty handed. A flock of golden plover darted by me as I stood up in the boat, and, sending a shot after them, I had the satisfaction of seeing two fall. Both tumbled into the reeds where the water was shallow, and what with the darkness, the ice round the reeds, and my boat being almost aground, I thought myself fortunate at the end of twenty minutes' hard work to find both birds.

When I had left the open water three-quarters of an hour previously, the breeze had just died away, leaving the surface of the lake smooth as glass, but my surprise was great on pushing out from the reeds to find a thin film of ice for a distance of forty or fifty yards. Without difficulty I sculled through this, but on nearing the *Tally*, which it will be remembered was moored up the river, found that between her and the lake was a considerable stretch of ice. This looked serious, so getting on board I immediately called a cabinet council to consider the position. There being good holding ground in the bay, we quickly determined to tow the yacht out beyond the margin of ice, and there anchor for the night, for we plainly saw that if we left her up the river, and the ice in the bay was to increase much in thickness, we might not be able to get out until the end of the frost.

All this was not accomplished without some little difficulty, as the decks were slippery from rime, and the anchor chain was covered with ice. I am afraid Sinbad and Hall indulged in a little grumble at having to shift their quarters, for probably nothing would have pleased them better than to see the *Tally* ice-bound for the rest of the winter. However, supper and a "dhrop of the crathure" set matters straight, and before we turned in, the "crew," Jim Hall, indulged us to one of his sympathetic ballads, sung with a rich Tipperary brogue which sounded pleasantly enough to our unaccustomed English ears. The song ended, we turned in, but slept badly, as the cold was intense.

The noise of the forehatch being pushed off in the morning awoke me, and I heard an exclamation followed by a whispering in the forecastle, and I thought I distinguished a sound suspiciously resembling a chuckle.

After a few minutes Sinbad came into the after cabin with a very long face.

"Begor, sir, we'll never get out of it, there is a power of ice round us."

You may believe me, D. and I were soon on deck after hearing this. The morning was bitterly cold. A slight fog hung over the lake, and certainly so far as we could see—about a hundred yards—was ice, but whether the whole lake was frozen or not we had no means of knowing.

"How thick is it?" asked I of Sinbad.

"Faith, I haven't looked to see," was his reply, "but it bears that gull, anyway."

Not more than twenty yards distant, and made so tame by the cold as to be perfectly regardless of us, stood a magnificent gull, one of the greater black-backs, in full winter plumage. I took a scull and progged at the ice, and found it required a heavy blow to break a hole through it. I never measured the exact thickness, but it was extraordinary for one night's frost, and I afterwards heard people were skating there the following day.

"What's to be done?" queried D.

"Arrah, never fear, your honour, I'll manage it for you," answered Sinbad with a look of satisfaction; "when we have had a bit of breakfast I'll make me way to Scarriff and get a car to take your honour to Youghal (our headquarters). Jimmy and me can get the auld *Tally* back into the river and settle her there for the winter."

But Sinbad overdid his part, and we saw through him. The hard weather had come at last, and we by no means intended to give up the shooting which would come with it. At present we could not tell if the ice extended beyond the bay; but during breakfast D. and

I determined to get the yacht out if possible. The meal over, I fastened an axe to a spare scull, and told Sinbad what we intended to do, directing him and Hall to get into the second boat, and side by side with us to break a passage through the ice. Our skipper's face fell, and a slight expostulation issued from his lips. Indeed, I almost expected mutiny to add to our troubles. But fortune favoured us. A gentle breeze coming from the west lifted the mist which overhung everything like a pall, and there, less than a quarter of a mile distant, were the blue open waters of the lake with a slight ripple upon them.

"Do you see that?" I pointed, triumphantly.

"I do, indeed; but we can't break through," answered Sinbad, stubbornly.

A little gentle sarcasm, however, had an excellent effect, especially a remark that he and Hall might go home in a car and leave us to smash a way through the ice and take the yacht to her moorings in Youghal Bay.

"I thought Irishmen had some pluck!" I concluded.

Without another word, Sinbad and the "crew" tumbled into one boat, D. and I into another, and soon we were working our hardest at the ice.

"It's a race who'll be through first!" I cried. "England against Ireland!"

I could not have made a better remark. The men were upon their mettle; they did their best, and, as they worked, their temper improved. Our progress was slow but sure. By eleven o'clock we had covered about half the distance, and success was certain. By twelve the race became exciting—England slightly leading. At 12.30 Ireland drew ahead, but soon got into difficulties, and for some time it was anybody's race. Finally, with a cheer, England's representatives broke through into the open water, the Irishmen following two minutes later.

But our work was not yet at an end. Turning our boat's noses towards the yacht, we began to make our way back through the broken ice, but had not gone far when we discovered that Dame Nature had performed a flank movement and made a vigorous attempt to outwit us. Our channel had frozen up again!—but not hard. In an hour or less we were back and on board. The anchor was quickly weighed, and in a very few minutes the *Tally* was being towed from her ice prison.

Our skipper had evidently decided in his own mind that we had done enough for glory, and so soon as we had towed the yacht well beyond the ice and gone on board, he set all sail and put her head in the direction of home, that is to say, the yacht's usual moorings in Youghal Bay.

"Sure it will be besht to get there," said he, "because the whole lake might freeze, and what would happen then if we were out in the middle of it?"

But a flock of plover which D. discerned on a low-lying island upset Sinbad's little homing schemes for the time being, for D., Hall and I at once jumped into the gig, and hoisting the sprit-sail sailed quietly down on the birds. All of us crouched low in the boat, Hall with just one hand over the gunwale to hold an oar to keep the little craft from running into the wind.

Kneeling on the bottom of a leaky boat—all Irish boats leak—is not pleasant work in winter, and more than once that afternoon I lost a good chance at duck by finding myself frozen to the floor-boards when rising to shoot. But to return to the plover. We were almost within shot when Hall suddenly changed the course of the boat. Cautiously peering under the sail, I soon saw the reason, for, right ahead of us, on a ledge of rock, were ten or a dozen pochards. We sailed on until they rose, when D. and I let fly almost together, but could not get a second shot, the sail being in the way. Away flew the plover with shrill pipings, down fell four of the pochards—two dead, two crippled. One of the latter gave us an exciting chase, but eventually all were secured.

Finding the birds so tame, we determined, our skipper notwithstanding, to shoot for the remainder of the afternoon, so, merely returning to the yacht for some food and directing Sinbad to keep us in sight, we worked our way in the little boat, sometimes sailing, sometimes rowing, in the direction of Holy Island. The frost had already wonderfully influenced the birds, and in many cases we were able to sail within easy reach of ducks and other wildfowl, and made a very fair bag.

Well content with what we had done, we were just starting to join the yacht, when we heard a great noise overhead, and, looking up, saw, not far above us, a large flock of wild geese. It was near dusk at the time, a few flakes of fine snow were falling, and the geese, usually so wary, appeared to take no notice of us. We kept still as death in the hopes that they would settle somewhere near, and were not disappointed, for they dropped on Holy Island, evidently intending to stay the night there.

"Can we get within shot of them?" I asked Hall.

"Faith, I don't know," replied that worthy in a whisper, "but we'll try, anyway."

Rowing cautiously round the island, we landed on the side most distant from the geese, and commenced a very elaborate stalk on hands and knees through about an inch of snow. Hall muttered something about the "good people" not liking mortals on the island after nightfall, and that they might inflict rheumatism on us for our invasion of their territory. The rheumatism I could believe in, but not the "good people," and told him so; but when he added that the cattle were "mortual wild," and he hoped "Tim Delaney's bull" was not anywhere about, I said nothing but maybe thought the more.

A weird, wild place is Holy Island on a winter's night, and our dismal and lengthy crawl gave us ample time for unpleasant reflections. But all these things must have an end, and we were getting nearer the geese every second, taking advantage of each bush and rock to keep ourselves from their keen eyes. Finally, D. and I reached the last available bush and found we were still some eighty yards or so from the birds, neither of us having larger shot than No. 1 in our barrels. What could be done? Obviously nothing, but to creep as near the geese as they would allow, and then fire. This we tried; but not two steps had we gone from the bush when the cackling ceased—the wary ones perceived us and took to wing. D. and I, of course, fired, and doubtless our small shot, at that distance, glanced off the thick plumage of the geese, and troubled them little more than the snow-flakes which were still falling. Though it was a wild-goose chase indeed, I confess I grieved over our disappointment somewhat, but was consoled two days later by shooting my first woodcock.

Disheartened by our bad fortune, we strolled slowly and sadly over the snow-covered, holy burying place, and the ruins of the churches, towards the boat, and were passing near the Round Tower, when we heard a noise such as would be made by a charge of cavalry. My nerves are fairly strong, but this tried them.

"It's the cattle!" screamed Hall, "run for it; they're divils when they're angry!"

But on a dark night, to run down a steep, rocky bank, its dangers hidden and aggravated by snow, is pretty nearly as bad as facing Tim Delaney's bull. Having a cartridge in my gun, I tried what a shot in the air would do. D. did ditto. The effect was magical. Up went the cattle's tails, down went their heads, and off they scampered into the darkness. Cattle are inquisitive. Not wishing to meet them when they recovered their nerves and returned to ascertain the why and wherefore of the flashes and objectionable noises, we hastened to the boat, picking up Hall by the way—he had rolled to the bottom of the bank—and pushed off from the rocky shore.

But where was the *Tallyhassie*?

We rowed hither and we rowed thither, but no yacht could we find. First one shouted, then the other, and then all three together, but met with no response. It had never occurred to the sapient Sinbad that we could not see in the dark, and having sailed into the middle of the lake to get plenty of sea room, if I may use the expression of fresh water, he put down the helm, let fly the jib sheets, hauled the foresail to windward, and warmed his toes in the forecastle, only now and again putting his head above the hatchway to see if we were coming.

We were in an anything but amiable frame of mind as we rowed vaguely about the lake, losing ourselves as soon as we lost sight of the island. After an hour and a half of this sort of thing, we tried a little gun-firing, but that had no effect, except perhaps to cause any peasants who heard the reports echoing across the water to draw the bedclothes over their heads and tremble, believing that Capt. Moonlight and his crew were abroad.

To be in the middle of a large lake on a very dark night searching about for a yacht which obstinately declines to show any lights, is one of the most hopeless and irritating performances imaginable. When the occupants of the boat are all weary as men can be after spending one half the day fighting their way through ice, the other half in sailing up wild fowl, and finally, wading on hands and knees through the snow over a good sized island, their feelings can, perhaps, be better imagined than described. Soon we became too tired even to shout, and considered the question of rowing to shore and seeking a night's lodging at the first cabin we could come across. But we were now out of sight of land and had no compass, so we were as likely to row ten or twelve miles up the lake to Ilanmore, or down it to Killaloe, as to make Mountshannon on the north or Derry on the south, neither of which could be more than a mile and a half distant. We had no food nor water in the boat, nor any wraps worth speaking of. Two ducks came flying close over our heads, and we were too spiritless to point a gun at them.

"I don't think muchof chasing wild geese," said D., "but I would sooner have twenty hunts after geese than one after a phantom yacht."

I silently concurred, for the position was becoming intolerable. "If we only had a light to wave about," said D., "the idea might screw itself into his stupid head that we were looking for him, and perhaps he might hang out a lantern."

But we had no light except a box of wax matches. As to these, one of us, I forget which, had a brilliant inspiration. Taking about half the box he shredded the stalks of the matches, tied them up into a sort of ball and fixed the combustible mass on the end of a piece of wood. At the moment Hall lit it D. and I fired off four shots as nearly as we could together. They seemed to us to make a terrible noise over the water. It was not the piffling little sound which modern smokeless powders make, but the good old report of strong black "Curtis and Harvey," the only ammunition which was obtainable on the lake-side. Hall waved the vesta-torch over his head. It burnt fiercely for about two minutes and then expired, and we waited results most anxiously, for it was our forlorn hope. We had just decided that we must take to the oars again and make for shore, when we saw a gleam of light in the distance. Fortunately for us, Sinbad heard the reports—I believe he was asleep up to that time—saw the fire, took the hint, and showed a light. In a quarter of an hour we were on board, and the west wind soon brought us to our moorings in Youghal Bay.

So ended a somewhat eventful day on Lough Derg.

The cranky, roomy old *Tally* is no more. She was broken up the following year—her owner having another yacht—and the last summer I spent in Ireland I saw her booby-hatch acting the ignominious part of roof to an aviary.

Commencing with Yacht Racing, and Ending with a Bag of Perch.

"O gallant striped with streamers gay
Like armour-plated ship of war
At anchor in some sunny bay,
And bristling o'er with mast and spar!
Thou'rt swift, like her, to chase a foe,
As prompt as she to seize a prize.
If one or far or near should show
Its presence to thine argus eyes."

COTSWOLD ISYS.

CHAPTER XI.

COMMENCING WITH YACHT RACING, AND ENDING WITH A BAG OF PERCH.

On Lough Derg is a small fleet of yachts, the queen of them at the time I am about to describe being the one on which I spent many happy months. In the summer we had some very interesting racing, though the wind had a way of absenting itself from the lake on the days fixed for regattas.

To see real enthusiasm one must visit an Irish race-course and hear the cries of the crowd as the "Tipperary" or "Galway Bhoy," as the case may be, wins. Coming next, and not long afterwards, is a local yacht race in which every owner is well known, and the crews consist of men who live round the lake.

"See now, it's Tim has got the rudder, his honour has gone below! Faith! now you'll see her move! Didn't I tell yer? See now, he's got the wind of her! Arrah, Tim's the bhoy!"—and men who have never boarded a more important sailing vessel than a turf boat in all their lives, wax as critical and enthusiastic as the keenest yachtsman who ever landed on the Squadron pier at Cowes.

We had regattas at Mount Shannon, Dromineer and Portumna, and, for those who cared to travel so far, at Athlone. The best of the yachts were undoubtedly the three and five tonners, but in a breeze none could approach the successor of the *Tallyhassie*. There was one year, however, in which she took no part in the Dromineer races, and I sailed from Mount Shannon to the bay in a little eighteen foot boat I had brought over with me from England, called the *Mouse*. She was cutter-rigged and fully decked in, a handy little craft which could go anywhere, do anything, and was as safe as a house. If needs be, one man, or even two, if they could stand a reasonable amount of stiflication, could sleep in her with more or less discomfort. So long as the wind was not quite strong enough to blow the stick out of her, she could go out on the lake, and I have seen her for an instant with two feet of water on her foredeck, the measurement being gauged by the knees of the lad who was forward freeing the foresheets, and who was all but swept overboard. Andy, however, was no great lover of the *Mouse*, and always set sail in her with great fear and trepidation.

* * * * *

There was a steady westerly wind blowing that August morning, which sent a rare swell rolling into Dromineer Bay, but the little craft rolled over the amber-coloured billows like a duck, though Andy looked uncomfortable. We cruised about the bay for some time and finally lay to just ahead of an old fifteen ton yacht, and waited to see the start of a very interesting race between some three tonners, one of which was a new boat.

The yacht astern of us was also lying to, but there was a crowd of people on board, including ladies, and I suppose the owner, who was at the tiller, was too much engaged with them to take the trouble to look ahead before putting up his helm and starting after the race.

However that may be, while I was watching the race through my binoculars Andy suddenly exclaimed, "Oh! begor! she's down on us!" and at that moment the bowsprit came straight over our stern, the bobstay catching me in the chest and sweeping me overboard. But the bobstay saved me the trouble of a swim, for I clung on to it, and after experiencing the sensations which must have fallen to the lot of witches in the olden times, who were placed in the ducking stool, for the yacht was plunging heavily in the swell, I managed to climb on board. I rather expect I was angry, but the owner took all the wind out of my sails and set me laughing by coolly hoping that I was not very wet? His son, however, showed a little more consideration. He took me on shore, gave me a dry rig-out, consisting of a red worsted nightcap and blue jersey, and rowed me back to the *Mouse*. We towed his punt astern while he sailed with us about half-way across the lake, and as bad luck would have it, he made fast our mainsheet by means of a most complicated knot.

The result was a mixture of the lamentable and

ludicrous. When rounding Hare Point, we had to bear away to avoid some rocks. Just then the wind strengthened considerably, and I found myself unable to release the knot of the mainsheet, which was close hauled. The *Mouse*, of course, heeled over, and for a few moments refused to answer the helm in the rough sea. Our lee-deck was a-wash, and the water all but entered the cockpit. Andy went down on his knees, produced a leaden talisman, which he wore round his neck, and began praying vigorously to the Virgin, after which he declared he would not sail an inch farther in the *Mouse*, but must be put ashore immediately. I did my best to allay his fears, but there was no help for it, and I had to put about, run before the wind, and come to an anchor in the shelter of the point. I had a minute Berthon boat in the cabin, and this we got out, and I took the timorous fellow ashore. He must have been a long time getting back to the yacht in which I had left my wife. Maybe he stopped to tell his troubles and drown them a little on the way. Somewhere about eleven o'clock he turned up, and made my wife think that I was as good as drowned, and that it would be a wonderful dispensation of Providence if she ever saw me any more!

Meanwhile, the weather was too wild for me to take the *Mouse* home by myself, so I lay at anchor all night in a desolate spot, and prayed that the wind would not change, and blow the *Mouse* ashore, for the bay in which I had moored her was open to the north-east. I feasted off a dry crust of bread, and before breakfast next day was strongly tempted with the end of a candle, the only other article in the nature of food on the *Mouse.*

But when I turned out in the morning, the wind had softened, and by eight o'clock I was back in Clonoolia Bay. I picked up the *Mouse's* moorings, then rowed to the yacht, which was lying a hundred yards off and got on board without anybody hearing me. I lifted a skylight and looked down into the cabin. There was my wife sleeping placidly enough; but immediately she awoke and saw an unshaven, red-faced ruffian wearing a red woollen nightcap gazing down upon her— well, she didn't recognise who it was, and what with the fears of the previous night and her resulting nervousness in the morning, there was a pretty to-do. However, things smoothed down after a while, as things usually do in this life, and I determined upon a quiet day at the moorings, with the result that I made friends with two very interesting fishermen.

While sitting lazily on the booby-hatch of the yacht, basking in the morning sunshine, and blinking over a well-thumbed yellow-back, I saw the men come sailing round the point in a small rowing boat, enter the bay, and behave in a manner which was mysterious, not to say suspicious. On reaching the shallows they lowered their little sprit-sail and one of them taking the sprit as a pole, stood on the very bows of the boat, a foot on each gunwale, and poled her along, peering intently in the amber-coloured water as he went. Presently he stopped the boat dead with a forward lunge of the little spar, backed her a few yards, and he and his companion quickly removed their boots and stockings and turned up their trousers and jumped into the water. The next proceeding was to take up the sprit-sail and one of the oars and apparently arrange them in the water in some peculiar fashion.

"Poachers," thought I at once; "well, it is not my business, but I shall see what they do."

Having fixed the sail to their satisfaction, one re-entered the boat and pulled round the shallow while the other waded, and soon it seemed as if they were driving something in front of them. At the end of various manœuvrings, which lasted about ten minutes, the wader made his way up to the sail and lifted up the corner of it, enclosing, I had no doubt, some fish. But what inhabitants of the lake, I wondered, would be so foolish as to be caught in this simple manner. Certainly not trout, nor pike, nor rudd. My curiosity excited, I jumped in to the dinghy and rowed across to the men, who greeted me in a friendly fashion, and without hesitation explained the reason of their proceedings.

It seems they were eel-fishers hailing from Athlone. Every summer they came down to Lough Derg with many hundred yards of eel lines and earned a precarious living by catching eels ranging mostly between half a pound to a pound and a half in weight (I suspect the very large eels broke away), despatching them alive in boxes to market at Liverpool. In the early part of the year they had to bait their lines entirely with worms called blueheads, but as soon as the weather warmed the little perch fry in vast numbers appeared on the shallows, and these they found infinitely better bait than anything they picked up out of the potato patches.

Bearing in mind that perch and eels are voracious fish, these hand-liners did really good service for the salmon and trout fishers, and were deserving of every encouragement. I was, therefore, not a little sorry to hear some time afterwards that an attempt was made, which I think was successful, to prohibit these lines being laid in Lough Rea.

Some days the eel boys took me in their boat, and they rigged me up a small line for my own use, which provided when required half a dozen or more delicate eels for use on the yacht; but not once did I see them catch anything except eels and an occasional perch, and on my little line which boasted twelve hooks, eels were the only fish caught.

It was a rough life these fellows led, their vocation taking them to the less frequented parts of the lake where lodgings were not obtainable, and many a night when the weather was reasonably fine did they sleep out on the islands under the shelter of alder, hazel, and furze bushes, or crouched under the lee of big moss and lichen-covered rocks when some sudden storm came hurrying along from the Atlantic not many miles distant. Often they would lay their lines on a calm quiet evening, and when in the morning they came to take them up again, there would be a terrible gale blowing, in which their little deal-built craft stood a good chance of foundering.

While one man rowed the other would take in the line, and unhook the eels with a dexterity which was simply marvellous. To the ordinary angler an eel is a fish of terror. It kinks his line, covers his clothes with slime, and in sheer desperation as often as not he cuts off its head or severs the line and leaves the cook to remove the hook. But it was rare indeed that these Irish eel-fishers had any difficulty in this connection. Immediately the eel was lifted up wriggling out of the water it was seized in the left hand, and before it had time to protest the case-hardened right thumb of the eel-man was down on the bend of the hook right in the eel's throat, a twist was given, out came the hook, and the eel seemed none the worse for the operation.

The exact method of catching the perch fry was as follows: The sprit-sail, used as a net, was brailed to the mast, which floated and supported it on one side. Two other sides of it were laid over the oars, while the fourth side was left open and sunk to the bottom by means of stones thrown upon it. The fry, which could be seen in shoals on the shallows, were then driven into the mouth of this simple trap, and a man standing in readiness lifted up the unfloated side of the sail and the baits were secured. The next portion of the operation was somewhat tedious, to wit, getting the water out of the sail, for the canvas was very nearly waterproof. This would take ten minutes or a quarter of an hour.

First of all the stones were removed, and gradually the depression in the sail was made smaller until the four or five hundred little fish swam about in a few quarts of water from which they were easily scooped out and placed in a pail. I have no doubt the perch fishing suffered from this destruction of the previous year's broods; but perch, and particularly eels, are most voracious fish, and the trout and salmon angler benefited.

For perch of average size there was no better bait than the perch fry of the size used to bait the eel-lines, and perhaps it will not be out of place here to write a few lines describing the perch and perch fishing of Lough Derg, a description which applies to several other large Irish lakes.

Those who condemn fresh water fish as food have surely never tasted well-conditioned perch from such a lough as Derg. These fish swim in the purest of water, over a bottom of gravel and rock, and feed on fresh water molluscs, the young of their own species, rudd and bream, and not a few baby trout. Taken fresh from the water, knocked on the head and promptly scaled, split open in two halves, boned, and fried in butter, they curl up in crisp freshness and eat solidly, jucily, and tenderly as any sole. I made it a rule whenever spending a few days at some sheltered moorings to hang out a big hamper over the stern of the yacht and keep it well stocked with live perch. Fish of the freshest and sweetest were then available for any meal, and were much appreciated by everyone on board.

These lake perch swim in shoals and run much of a size. Inshore, on the shallows, the infants of last year cruise about in thousands, in at most a couple of feet of water. At a depth of three or four feet, when the sun shines brightly, looking down through the amber-coloured water, a shoal of larger fish will often pass by, the individual members of which run about three or four inches in length. As the water deepens, the fish parade, owing to the peat stain, becomes more or less a vanishing quantity. But moor the dinghy close by a thick bed of weeds in two fathoms of water, fish with suitable tackle and baits, and surely, if the conditions are right, a couple of dozen third-of-a-pounders will be hauled up kicking into the boat in the course of an hour. In the still deeper water, say about three and a half to four fathoms, which is the depth most fished, the perch run half-a-pound to three-quarters, though here an occasional large one may be expected. But the really fine perch must be sought after in about four fathoms or more of water, and the most attractive bait is something larger than worm or perch fry.

In the Shannon lakes the bait which is considered " great medicine " for large perch by the fishermen is (tell it not in Gath !) a small trout ! The Irish peasant has no mercy where game of any kind is concerned, but will take the parent trout off the spawning beds in winter without the least remorse, and in spring and summer may be seen hunting over the shallows of the river for the yearlings wherewith to bait his pike and perch lines.

But, after all, to sacrifice a trout to catch a perch or pike is not so very iniquitous a proceeding as may appear at first blush, for if Master Perch or Sir Esox Lucius, which by this means is destroyed, were allowed to extend its days it would assuredly live on the fat of the water and destroy thousands of salmonidæ. Thus the yearling trout used as bait dies the death of a martyr in the noble cause of salmon and trout preservation.

But to return to the big perch. Armed with a couple of dozen small trout, which swim unconscious of their impending, unpleasant, but noble fate in water-can or bucket, the local fisherman ventures out into as deep water as he can find bearing weeds, moors by some aquatic kitchen garden and, fishing with a hook large enough to catch a salmon, sits and waits, and after a while hauls up a perch which may weigh anything between 1½lb. and 3lb. Needless to say, these large fish are not so plentiful as those of smaller size, but the reward and satisfaction in catching them are greater.

Taking size and numbers in consideration I never enjoyed better perch fishing than in Lough Derg, but even there, thinly populated as the country was and is, there was a vast difference in the fishing grounds lying anywhere within a mile of humanity and those off some barren shore, unapproachable except by means of yacht or, at least, a sea-worthy rowing boat. Those comparatively unapproachable waters were, it need hardly be said, the best from the angler's point of view. Mick was a great believer in a remote portion of the lake known as Coos Bay. It was an awkward place for us, as it afforded no safe anchorage for the yacht. The fish bit best in the early morning and late evening, and one had either to sail to the place at night or leave it some time after sundown. This I never liked doing, except in bright moonlight, for though the channels of this rocky lake are fairly well buoyed, there are no beacons to guide the navigator after nightfall. I therefore never gave the fishing at Coos Bay a really good trial, but one mild August evening, a day or two after the Dromineer yacht races, I had there one of those pieces of sport which the enthusiastic angler ever looks back upon with the keenest pleasure.

The morning had been sunny and bright, and Mick and I devoted ourselves to catching perch fry, for these were our standing bait, and, as I have said, very superior to the worms used by the Irish, and called "blueheads."

For some reason or other, probably because they had been harried by the eel boys, the young of the perch were disinclined to come over the spritsail which we lowered under water for their special benefit; but before lunch time we had obtained enough for our purpose, quickly got under way, and were carried by a soft, southerly breeze up to Coos Bay.

As soon as the anchor had been let go, and everything made snug, we jumped into the fishing boat which we had towed behind, and Mick brought me to a great patch of weeds standing out in the lough about a furlong from the shore. It was a desolate spot. Bare rocks showed up above the surface. Here and there the stony shores were fringed with a scanty growth of reeds, and rolling moorlands trended up from the water's edge. Not a tree, nor, if I remember aright, even a cotter's hut, broke the monotony of Lord Clanricarde's great peat bogs. A few wild ducks, with their broods of flappers, swam about, and now and again a grey crow would come down to the water's edge and search for such food as the barren shore afforded.

The local method of catching perch is to have one or two hooks at the end of a fine hemp line, with a lead (as likely as not, cut off a piece of composition piping, or the sheeting used on roofs), placed a foot or two above them. I found our ordinary English paternoster answer far better than this rough contrivance, and very soon had one overboard, baited with two small perch, each about an inch long.

In sending the paternoster smartly through the water, an experienced hand can feel when the lead hits the bottom, and even judge whether that bottom be of rock, or sand, or mud. But on this occasion I was puzzled to know what the bottom was like, for the feeling of the lead was different to anything I had ever experienced. But there was a bite almost immediately, and, reeling up, I found I had two perch, each of about three-quarters of a pound, on my paternoster. That was a good beginning, and, without much doubt, the brace of fish flew at the bait before the lead reached the bottom at all. Mick smiled, as he always did when our endeavour bore fruit, quickly re-baited my hook, and down went the paternoster again among the shoal.

This time the lead was allowed to reach the bottom, but no sooner was it resting than there came that pleasant double knock on the end of the rod, and, striking, I found I was in another fish. And so the sport went on, sometimes one, sometimes two fish being brought into the boat at once, and, at the end of two hours, I had six dozen as fine perch as an angler could reasonably desire. Few, if any, were under half a pound, but, I believe, none were over a pound; the majority were three-quarter-pounders. Suddenly there came a subtle, curious, and indefinable change in the atmospheric conditions. It was not colder, nor had the wind shifted so far as I could see, but I made a remark on the subject to Mick, saying I should not be surprised if the fish left off biting now there was some change in the weather coming.

My prophecy of evil was verified, for never another bite came to me that evening, the fish leaving off as suddenly as they commenced. But what reasonable being can wish for more than seventy-two perch, mostly over half a pound each, in a short evening's fishing?

Rudd versus Medicine Man.

"*Like a rose-leaf thy fins, and thy scales like the pearl,
Thou'rt dowered with beauty, arrayed like an earl;
When fresh from the stream, on the grass thou doth lie
Thy manifold grace is a feast for the eye.*"

COTSWOLD ISYS.

CHAPTER XII.

RUDD versus MEDICINE MAN.

MEDICINE men most of us know, but to the many no definite meaning attaches to the word "rudd."

The rudd then, let it be explained, is a fish so called, perhaps, because of its fins and eyes of ruddy hue. It is one of those creatures which, in an age when the higher education of fish is seriously undertaken by the disciples of the dry-fly, roach pole, and others, still retains a simple-mindedness which, combined with a confiding disposition, has led to its destruction—nay, I may say total obliteration, in many waters, the Thames to wit. But it is still to be found in the Bedfordshire Ouse, the broads of Norfolk and Suffolk, and not a few small lakes and ponds.

In Ireland the roach is not. Pat, however, will tell you I am mistaken, for rudd, which are most abundant in the Sister Isle, are called locally "roach." In no place are these fish more plentiful than in the fair lough of happy memories, on which I spent so many days of my life. There they may be caught on ordinary float-tackle, using worm or paste on the hook. In hot weather they come on to the shallows and give good sport to the fly-fisher. Sometimes they are pisciverous (sweet word! meaning fish eating) for when baiting my hook with a baby perch I once caught a large rudd.

Ay, but what is a rudd? Imagine a portly roach, rather deep and aldermanic as to its corporation, with tail deeply forked and fins and eyes of bright red, the dorsal fin being set well back and nearer the tail than on the roach proper. Imagine such a fish, I say, and you have a picture of a rudd in your mind's eye. Truly with small fish it is a little difficult to distinguish between the two species, but the following test is infallible. Seize the upper lip of the fish under examination and try to pull it down towards the under lip. If you find no lip to speak of, merely a bony and immovable substance, the fish is a rudd. If on the other hand the lip is gristly and may be extended downwards, we have a roach. From this it may be surmised that the roach is more of a bottom feeder than the rudd.

But let me to my little story of the doctor and the rudd, for these descriptions of fish are apt to weary the "general reader," who, ranking among my best friends, I feel bound to honour and study in every possible way.

A message was delivered to me on board the yacht that the doctor was coming. Two days previously I had been rather unwell, and expressed a wish to see the medicine man of the district. Now I was better, and felt rather in the position of one who, forced by toothache to visit his dentist's, on arriving at the chamber of horrors, finds himself more or less free from pain, and exceedingly loth to undergo the odious operation, for which an hour ago he was so anxious. However, the doctor was coming, and I must see him; so telling my man that I should not want him until lunch time, I resigned myself to a lounge on deck in the sunshine.

It was one of those days, so rare in Ireland, when the sun pours down with full midsummer force; were such days more frequent, we should hear less of the troubles of Irish peasants and Scotch crofters. The broad Shannon looked very beautiful that morning. In the distance the round tower and the ruins on Holy Island were reflected in the still water, and more to the right I could just discern the rocky shores along which Charles O'Malley sailed for his life after his famous duel. Not a sound was to be heard, save the cooing of wood pigeons in the larch wood which lined the rocky shores of the bay, and now and again the whistling cries of merry little dabchicks disporting at the edge of the great reed beds some hundred yards or so from the yacht.

I was just getting interested in one of Samuel Lover's tales of Irish peasant life, when my man, who had been rambling along the shore in search of firewood, came on board in a state of excitement, with the news that great shoals of fish were swimming about on the shallow behind the reed bed. Would I cast a fly over them? To this I said "certainly," provided he would tell me what the fish were. He did not quite know. Anyway, they were not trout; some people called them roach, and the captain once caught a pailful with his fly rod.

That last remark was enough for me, and in a very few minutes I had my ten-foot Farlow in fighting order and was very quietly poling the dinghy over the shallow towards the reed bed behind which were the "roach."

I soon reached the spot, and there was a shoal of fish, indeed—the water seemed alive with them. Mooring the dinghy to the edge of the reeds I put up one moderate-sized fly, a governor, dressed after the late Mr. Francis's pattern. My first cast yielded somewhat astonishing results. Every fish within a circle of ten yards seemed bent on taking the fly, and there was a general rush for it. I struck at once and hooked nothing. When next my little governor went flying through the air and alighted near the shoal, I profited by experience, and let the fly rest until the line tightened a little, then struck, and hooked a good fish. I gave him the butt strongly, for the bottom was smothered with a thick mass of weeds, which came to within about six inches of the surface. There was in consequence a good deal of kicking and plunging, and I was not sorry to see his gleaming bronze side turn up to the sunlight. I soon had him on board, and my roach proved to be a handsome rudd of about 2lb. weight. I quickly caught others, not quite so large, but after two or three had been landed, the shoal would leave the shallow for a few minutes, only to return to go through the same performance.

The rudd does not, as a rule, rise like a trout. The

fly should be cast as near the fish as possible, allowed to sink a few inches, and then be drawn slowly through the water. A slowl swirl coming towards it shows the approach of a decent fish which may or may not suck in the lure and be duly brought to basket. One is very apt to strike too soon, especially if accustomed to trout fishing. The best plan is to watch the line carefully and to strike the moment it begins to straighten out.

My first fish was not the only two-pounder I caught that morning, and by twelve o'clock I had some twenty or more handsome rudd kicking about the bottom of the dinghy, for in my hurry I had brought neither basket nor landing net. About that time my man hailed me that the doctor was on the quay waiting to come aboard; but as at least the whole College of Surgeons would have been required to induce me to leave such a good bit of fishing, I shouted word back that I was exceedingly busy, and begged he would excuse me for awhile.

The shoal, which had been taking one of its periodic cruises in the deeper water, made its reappearance, and the antics of a large rudd which seemed to have strong conscientious objections to keep out of the weeds when hooked, caused me to forget for awhile all about my would-be medical attendant. In a few minutes, however, I espied him, escorted by Captain S., scrambling over the rocks towards me. Captain S. was a fisherman, so took in the whole state of affairs at a glance; but the doctor seemed a trifle annoyed when he discovered the "business" which had caused me to delay making his acquaintance.

However, he sat down on a rock and quietly waited, watching me. I had not previously caught so many heavy fish with the fly in so short a time. But then these fish were absolutely unsophisticated, and took the fly greedily. There were, of course, some small ones, but the large majority weighed over half a pound.

At the end of half an hour I felt I could not decently keep the worthy disciple of medicine waiting any longer, so took him on board, and had to explain that an angler may, under certain circumstances, have a somewhat quick pulse without it denoting disease of any kind. Then he went away, remarking that he really did not see the necessity of sending me any medicine at present. There had been no time to wash out the dinghy, and as I bade farewell to the doctor at the quay I noticed that his trousers glittered like a harlequin's dress, the spangles being some hundred or more scales from defunct rudd.

That evening there was a great distribution of fish among the peasantry, one of whom assured me that rudd were "grand eating entoirely."

A more or less modern hunting song propounds the axiom that there is "only one cure for all maladies sure," which is, "the sound of the horn on a fine hunting morn;" but I venture to assure the writer that thirty rudd, weighing 30lb., caught in two hours and a half, is to some persons a better cure for most of the diseases to which flesh is heir than the sound of a thousand horns, or even a blue pill.

The Forty Pound Pike.

"*O Lucius esox! beware of the day
When Nemesis comes in an angler's array!
He, too, can be cunning! beware like Lochiel,
Of his arm which shall strike with the conquering steel.*"

COTSWOLD ISYS.

"*Fathers and guardians were commanded to teach the male children the use of the long-bow.*"

GREENER.

CHAPTER XIII.

THE FORTY POUND PIKE.

Our old friend the forty pound pike of Ireland may, and probably does, exist. He may even have been caught, but his alleged captures do not so far bear investigation. I would strongly advise persons who land these monsters to say nothing as to length and girth. Many a forty pounder would have had place in history had not the captor given these particulars, and thus thrown doubt and discredit on a story in which he would otherwise have figured as hero.

A striking peculiarity of these great pike is that their bodies are never preserved. One I investigaged—it was a fifty pounder by the way—had been given to the pigs; another, which was even larger, had been torn to pieces by dogs. Surely such venerable fish deserved a nobler fate, and far be it from me to suggest that had their illustrious corpses been produced, their weights would have been found wanting. However, he who being a pike fisherman has not a yarn of a monster up his sleeve is no true angler, so, for my credit's sake, I feel bound to spin one. Whether it will bear the strictest investigation, is not for me to say. But do I not produce the photo of the fish, taken from life, which is something?

* * * * *

The situation was not a pleasant one. During a long tramp after snipe over the bog, a sea fog came up from

"THE POOR SHELTER OF A SHEBEEN."

the Atlantic obscuring all things; I hopelessly lost my way, and, instead of joining in the pleasant Christmas festivities at Ballyracket Hall, found myself only thankful enough to have the poor shelter of a shebeen for the night. Whether Pat was keeping Christmas at home, or

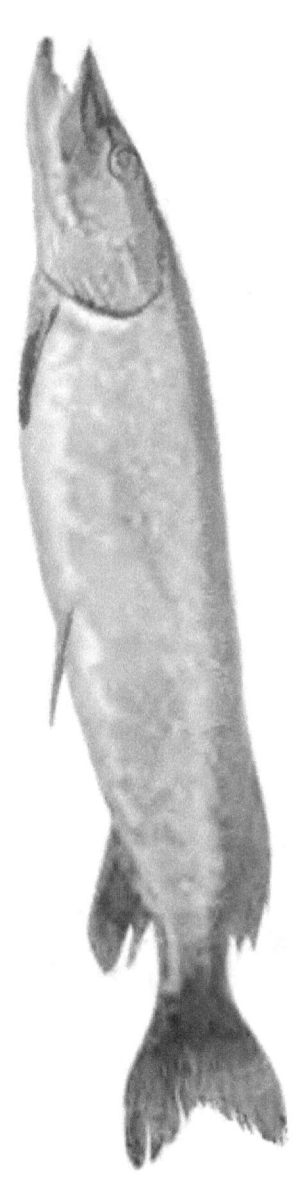

THE FORTY POUND PIKE.   201

simply objected to venture out in the fog, I know not. However, that may be, the worthy woman who sold unlicensed whisky, and her grandson, a bare-legged gossoon, were the only people in the cabin besides myself.

The boy had no English worth speaking about; the woman had too much, and her rattle wearied me, so after the first ten minutes I sat glumly watching the large iron pot which was suspended from a hook over the peat fire on the open hearth. The said pot contained my supper—a mixture of chicken, rabbit, onion, potatoes, cabbage, and a herring thrown in. I had protested mildly against the herring, but protests were unavailing with Mrs. O'Day who only said that I was to "lave it" to her. I was too tired to argue the point, so "laved it" accordingly.

After all, the place was not so bad. Those peat embers threw out a most agreeable warmth, and the fine odour of Irish stew was a really pleasant stimulus to the appetite of a hungry man. Truly I could have felt more at home if the cow had not been moored at the other end of the room; and those chickens on the rafters—well, I was careful not to sit beneath them. But it was a thousand times better than a night in the bog with such poor shelter as a peat stack might afford. And I was in no critical mood.

As I sat steaming in the attempt to dry myself before the peat fire, the blue, scented smoke from which coiled and collected among the rafters, my eyes lit on a fishing rod which stood in the corner of the room. There was a reel attached to it. Now, there is nothing remarkable in seeing a rod and reel in Ireland, but these particular weapons made me open my eyes and mouth with amazement. The rod at its point was thick as my little finger, the reel not less than 8in. in diameter, and the line — shade of Izaak Walton! What a line was there! I have towed a canoe up the Thames with cord less thick.

I was on the point of inquiring into the particular uses of this remarkable tackle, when the door of the cabin opened, and a short, wiry old man, with deep-set, piercing eyes, iron-grey hair, and clad in a shabby suit of tweeds, came in wearily, bearing just such another rod and reel, and a huge basket which I instinctively felt contained fish. He took no notice of me, but gasped out, in a voice which told of his exhausted condition, "The steelyard! the steelyard!"

With trembling hands he opened the rush basket and turned out of it one of the largest pike I had ever seen. Mrs. O'Day, who seemed in no way surprised, produced an ancient, rusty instrument, and proceeded in a business-like manner to weigh the fish. The old man's excitement while she did this was painful to witness. "Is it? is it?" he commenced.

"No, begor! it isn't," said Mrs. O'Day, calmly. "He's 5lb short."

I was looking at the fish, but, hearing a groan, turned my eyes to the old fisherman, and saw him lying on the floor of the shebeen. He had fainted.

THE FORTY POUND PIKE.

"Poor ould man," said Mrs. O'Day, it's disappointed he is—and wake, too, for divil a bit of food has he touched this day since yesterday. Undo his collar, sor, and sprinkle the face of him with a drap of wather. Deed, then, but I'll mix him a timperance drink. There's the milk fornint ye. Patsy, see if the ould hen hasn't left an egg in that corner, that's a good lad."

And so her tongue ran on. Meanwhile, the old fellow came to himself and sat up, but his eyes went at once to the pike, which still lay on the floor.

"Only 35lb!" I heard him mutter to himself. "But I will have him soon, I will have him soon now."

Mrs. O'Day's "timperance drink" was in the nature of egg flip. Beat up an egg in a quarter of a pint of whiskey, add a quarter of a pint of hot milk, and you have a reviving combination which is at once pleasant to the palate, nourishing to the body, and stimulating to the nerves. It acted like a charm on the old man, who five minutes after drinking it rose, kicked the fish to the side of the cabin, and for the first time appeared to be aware that a stranger was in the shebeen. Mrs. O'Day noticed the questioning look which he cast at me.

"It's a gintleman who losht his way in the bog," she said.

"Not fishing?" he asked, rather anxiously.

"No, snipe shooting," said I, and he seemed to me greatly relieved at the intelligence.

Mrs. O'Day now turned out the stew on to a large dish, and apologised for having no plates, remarking that she was "not used to the gintry, but maybe a saucer might do instead." We were both of us more or less famished, and talked but little during the meal, after which, Mrs. O'Day having provided us with a second edition of the "timperance drink," we drew the settle close to the peat fire, and commenced to chat over our pipes.

My new acquaintance, from what I could gather, was an Englishman who had lived for many years in Ireland, and apparently passed his whole time in fishing; but I was able to tell him of certain modern methods of pike fishing of which he had heard nothing. By-and-by he began to get communicative, and finally I ventured to ask him why the weighing of the pike had so disturbed him. Without hesitation he told me the following story:

"From a boy," said he, "I was an enthusiastic fisherman. I need not trouble to tell you now how I caught salmon in Norway, gudgeon in the Thames, trout in the Test, and enormous grayling in the Hampshire Avon. I fished whenever and wherever I could, and nothing, however large or however small, came amiss to me. But one thing I had never caught—a really large pike. Even in Sweden I never took one over 30lb. This nettled me, for many were the tales I read of monsters, particularly in the Irish lakes. One morning I read in a sporting paper a letter from an Irishman—a tackle dealer, so I afterwards ascertained—asking why English anglers did not come more over there. In the lakes in his neighbourhood there was fine pike fishing. Thirty-pounders were common, and they got a forty-pounder or two every season. Here was exactly the information I wanted. I told some friends about it, but they only smiled. I said I would catch a forty-pounder before long. They replied that there was no such thing as a forty-pounder alive or stuffed. Well, the end of it was I made a bet that I would go to Ireland and before I returned I would catch a fish of that weight."

I here interrupted his story to tell him of a strange coincidence. It was that very tackle-maker's letter which had first brought me to Ireland. "But go on," I said. "Finish your story and then you shall have mine."

"I began badly," he continued. "I wrote to the man for details of these loughs he mentioned, and received a reply from his widow, he having died soon after writing the paragraph. From the poor woman I could get no information. She said she had no idea to which waters her husband referred; in fact, she knew of none. Then I put a letter of inquiry in the sporting papers, and received many replies from persons, some of whom were possibly not altogether disinterested in the matter."

"I have suffered in the same way myself," I interjected.

"I came to Ireland armed with tackle such as would hold the largest pike that ever lived," he continued, not noticing my interruption. "At first I was hopeful. What tales they told me, to be sure! There was one of a big pike caught in Lough Derg, or, I should say, was killed by some workmen who were digging drains near the lake. The Bishop of Killaloe was reputed to be fond of pike, and to him the fish was taken. It was so large that half its body dragged on the ground as two men carried it, slung on a pole, to the bishop's palace. When the bishop saw it, he told them to give it to the pigs. 'I am fond of pike,' said he, 'but distinctly decline to have anything to do with sharks.' Ah! what would I not have given to have caught that fish!

"Well, I fished here and I fished there, first trying all the large Shannon lakes, and then visiting Corrib and Cullen. Thence I went to the North of Ireland, catching now and then some fine fish, but never even a thirty-pounder. The more difficult I found it to attain my object, the more determined I became to succeed. Ay, and I shall succeed yet, too! Let me see; it is now twenty-five years since I came to Ireland. Why, I must have killed thousands of pike in that time. That one there is the largest of the lot; in fact, the largest I have seen killed by myself or anyone else. This is my second great disappointment. At Athlone I thought I had succeeded. That *was* a big fish. We took him to the station, and weighed him there. 'Forty-three pounds,' said the station-master.

"A Major Browne, who was looking on, began to prod the fish with his stick. 'Something hard there,' said he; 'let's cut him open and see what he had for dinner.'

"I would not agree to this, as I wanted the skin entire; but the Major squeezed him a bit, and up came a lot of swan-shot which my scoundrel of a boatman had evidently poured down his throat so that he might earn the reward I had promised him if I caught a heavy fish. But at last I really have found a monster pike—the catching of him is only a question of time. Not a quarter of a mile from this cabin" (here he lowered his voice to a whisper) "is a deep, reedy lake. The priest has a boat on it, which he lends me. I was rowing along the other evening, when something struck the boat with such force that I was thrown from the seat and nearly capsized. It was in deep water, and there are no rocks in the lake. I had rowed right on to a pike as large as a calf."

He said the last sentence slowly and earnestly. I expect I showed great interest in the statement, for, like the old man, it had long been my ambition to catch a really immense pike. "Well," said I, "let us go and try the lake together; I should like to help you land such a monster."

"Ah! but you might catch him and not I. How then?" and he gave me a very unpleasant look out of his deep set eyes.

We said nothing for awhile, when my companion suddenly startled me by asking if I was aware that he was the Emperor of Germany. I said I was not, and another unpleasant silence ensued. Mrs. O'Day had made up two heather beds for us on the mud floor, and without undressing we each stretched ourselves on our moorland couches. Just as I was dropping off to sleep, my companion got up on his elbow and said gravely:

"Hang me if I don't believe you're a pike. I'll have a triangle into you to-morrow morning. Good-night!"

There was no doubt of it; he was mad. I dared not go to sleep. I made a pretence of it until the old man began to snore, which he soon did with much vigour, and then sat up by the fire until daybreak, when, leaving some money on the table for the voluble Mrs. O'Day, I sped away over the moor in the direction of Ballyracket Hall.

Years afterwards I was telling the tale of the demented angler, who, I felt certain, had lost his wits in his unavailing search after a big Irish pike, when I was interrupted by that vulgar fellow, Rooney, of the Irish bar, who burst into a peal of laughter, swearing that he knew my pike-fishing acquaintance well, and that there was no saner man in Ireland. "Fact is, Johnny," said he, "the old boy was fearful you would get that big fish before him, and so thought he would frighten you home."

Rooney may say what he likes, but I decline to believe in the sanity of any man who expatriates himself during a quarter of a century in the endeavour to catch a forty-pound pike.

"Tempest Toss'd."

*"So may the words I write
Tell through what storms I stray."*

MOORE.

"Now would I give a thousand furlongs of sea for an acre of barren ground; long heath, brown furze, anything: The wills above be done! but I would fain die a dry death."

THE TEMPEST.

*"Yet a greater space
To us had been grace,
For still as we neared the shore,
The wild white roll of the waves on the shoal
Roared round us more and more,
Roared out, in a ring around us,
You might see them fore and aft,
On ragged ledge,
And splintered edge,
All mad to dash our craft."*

EDWIN ARNOLD.

CHAPTER XIV.

"TEMPEST TOSS'D."

I was staying for a week in a house on the borders of the lake, and was curious to know the reason a great bar of wood about six inches square stood in a corner of my bedroom.

"Faith, whin it blows," said Eileen, "wouldn't the winders be bursht in if we didn't place an obstrooksion across thim same?"

I found afterwards that every window on the south-west side of the house was furnished with a similar bar for use whenever the Atlantic sent the lake one of its periodic gales. I am afraid I rather laughed at this excess of caution, which was particularly noteworthy in such a happy-go-lucky country, where the people love to "run chance"—to use an Irishism.

Large lakes are usually reputed stormy places, but those who visit them in spring and summer are apt to take a certain discount off the stories told by the natives of the fierce tempests which sometimes rage over waters then so softly rippling. But though months may pass without the Storm-King waving his wand over this or that lake, sooner or later comes a tempest the mere memory of which makes strong men shudder.

Lough Derg is certainly one of the most wind-swept sheets of water in Ireland. Storms tear across the Atlantic unchecked, whirl in and out and round about the mountains and higher moorlands of Kerry, Clare, and Galway, and with their fury almost as great as on the open sea, beat down upon the lough, and particularly on the few miles of water immediately above its outfall.

One July morning I had a famous taste of a Killaloe tempest. I had arrived over night at the cathedral fishing village. The yacht which I had hired of a friend, who lived some ten miles up the lake, was to have met me the following morning. A great wind awoke me. From my bedroom window I saw things flying in the air over the rushing Shannon, and people were swaying as they walked across the old bridge. I dressed and hastened down stairs. Would the yacht be round, I asked.

"Divil a yacht would lave her moorings in such a wind," was the reply; and I could well believe it.

After breakfast, as I looked out from the windows of the Royal Hotel, I saw a young woman with a yoke across her shoulders, from which depended two pails, coming down the grassy slope on the other side of the river to get water. The pails swung to and fro, the wind took liberties with her petticoats, and she seemed in real danger of being blown off her feet. But she got to the margin of the river, and knelt down. She filled her pails, stood up, and then this fierce, whimsical wind played the prettiest juggling trick imaginable. Taking first one pail up, then the other, it emptied them to the last drop, and she, laughing, for many were looking on, ran up the bank waterless. A wind that could play such pranks with a sweet Irish maiden would, I felt sure, have little mercy on a yacht, and I knew that my cautious skipper would not be likely to put to sea in such weather.

About mid-day the gale actually increased, and roaring up the river, uplifted in the air the water, on which the sun, shining brightly, imprinted a dazzling rainbow. In the afternoon I determined to drive to Youghal, where lived the owner of the yacht. It was a wild drive indeed. The road for some miles was sentinelled with great elms. Quite half of these were prostrate, but owing to the slant of the wind, had fallen at an angle, and there was just room for the car to pass between the hedge and the topmost branches. About the time I reached Youghal the wind changed, and blew a number of trees straight across the road, forming an impassable baricade, with the result that the car-driver was unable to return to Killaloe that night.

I went down to the quay to look at the yacht. She was pitching in the great swell which came rolling into the bay, every now and again her bowsprit dipping into the foaming water. The wind was blowing up the lake, and so great was its force that it held back the water and caused a flood on the higher reaches of the Shannon which, as I have explained, runs through the lough. The hay was out in the fields at the time, and many tons of it were washed away; but that on the hill-side fared no better, for the haycocks were lifted up like feathers and scattered over the wild waters. Next morning when I went aboard, the lake was placid as any mill pond, but the fringe of sodden hay along the side was as seaweed on the sea-shore.

There is no more dangerous craft to be out in during a storm than an open boat. My worst experience of the kind was on a fair June morning, a hot, sunny day, hardly a cloud to be seen, a gentle breeze rippling the water, the Mayflies scudding across the surface, big trout rising here and there, swallows chasing the May-flies, and solemn, grey crows stalking about the shore picking up the delicate morsels as they were blown off the water. To the northward the rolling moorlands rose to a considerable height, and on their summits were a few fleecy white clouds which certainly portended no storm. Most fortunately, as it turned out, I was in a well-built boat with a right sturdy oarsman.

We were about three hundred yards from the shore, and on the other side of us, and about equally distant, was a small island of an acre or less in extent. Beyond the island the lake stretched away for a couple of miles or more.

Suddenly there came from the shore a blast which turned the whole of the lough white with foam. The water being somewhat shallow, the violence of the wind raised up rows of breakers which curled over

ON THE HIGHER MOORLANDS.

all around us. Such a sight may be seen any day at low water when a heavy gale is blowing on a flat, sandy shore.

Mick turned the boat's head towards the little stone quay and pulled manfully, but not an inch could he move her; in fact, we were rapidly being carried astern towards the centre of the lake, so great was the force of the wind. Had we been forced out on to the deep open water where the seas were heavy and the spindrift was flying, and where, of course, the wind was very much greater than near the shore, I think we should have been swamped in about a minute.

The island saved us. It was evidently no use for Mick to attempt to regain the quay, and so great was the wind that I dared not take an oar, for had the man stopped rowing to enable me to change my seat, we should have been twisted round and blown over in an instant.

"Don't stop pulling," said I, quietly, "but let her drop astern. Work her as near the island as you can, and as soon as we have passed it row up under its lee."

Mick, as I have said, was a good oarsman, and carried out my orders to the letter, though just as we passed the island it seemed for a minute or two as if we should be swep on, for the low, scrubby growth gave but scant protection against the fearful gale that was blowing. And the strange thing about it was that within a quarter of an hour or even less, the wind had spent its fury. Half an hour later the wind had died away, and the scene regained its placid, summer-like beauty.

After Mick had refreshed himself—and well he deserved a refresher!—we started off dapping, and had some fairly good sport towards the evening. All through this curious storm there was no sign in the sky to indicate the quarter from which the wind was blowing, or that there was any great atmospheric disturbance taking place.

* * * * *

The mountain-surrounded arm of the lough which leads up to Killaloe often appeared to contain a choice and powerful collection of all the winds that blew. Sometimes when a mile or two distant from the mouth of this natural funnel, and floating in an absolute calm, I have seen the water foaming as the wind rushed out from it and across the lake, and large yachts heeling over as they were struck by the squall. I was destined to have a terrible experience of the same kind myself before long; but of that more anon. One summer, while living on the sixteen tonner, I had, as I have said in an earlier chapter, a small cutter yacht, called the *Mouse*, which nowadays would be termed a one-rater. She was a handy and quick means of getting about the lake. She was almost fully decked, and more seaworthy than the modern small racing craft. In fact, no greater harm was likely to happen to us than being blown ashore, or losing some of our spars. It had to be bad weather, indeed, to keep the *Mouse* at her moorings.

One day, being in want of provisions badly, I set sail

in the little craft with the object of getting to the shops at Killaloe. There was not much wind on the open lake, but as soon as we passed the island which guards the mouth of Killaloé reach (if I may so term it), we met a strong and squally head wind, which raised up a big, and at the same time, short sea, into which the nose of the *Mouse* plunged heavily. It is a small thing to take a green wave on board the turtle-deck which protects the bows of a big steamer, but in an eighteen foot boat, a passing visit from a comparatively modest billow created considerable pother. I had a lad with me, a native of a Thames-side town, and several times that afternoon he was clinging on to the mast to save himself from being swept overboard, the water, as it rolled over the deck, actually reaching up to his knees. It was quite the nastiest bit of sailing I ever experienced, and my youthful crew from the Thames was not a little alarmed.

Twice we all but went ashore, for the short, high waves so checked the way on the little vessel that she would not go about. We made but little progress, and terrible squalls came down from the hills every few minutes. Finding that even if I made Killaloe I should not have time to get back to Mount Shannon before darkness set in, I went about and bore away for home under the foresail only.

*   *   *   *   *   *

Once only was I caught in a really furious storm when aboard the yacht, and of all the terrible and anxious experiences I have ever suffered when on angling expeditions, that was perhaps the greatest. We were moored with two anchors in Clonoolia, or Priest's bay, which is usually deemed one of the safest corners of the lake. On the east the land encircles it and, at its mouth, trends round to the westward. On the opposite shore a pine-clad point projects some distance, and the entrance to the bay which faces the south is partly blocked by a low, rocky island. The opening through which boats, yachts, and, alack! storms can enter is only thirty or forty yards wide. As we lay in this almost land-locked anchorage we could look through the small opening across some two or three miles of water as far as the mouth of that stormy arm of the 'lough which leads up to Killaloe.

One evening early in September I went on deck just before turning in, and looked around. The lake was as a looking-glass, the sky bright and clear. Never was scene more peaceful; never was there a more striking absence of tempestuous weather signs.

But a storm must have been even then gathering among the mountains around Killaloe, the like of which that century had not seen. We turned in, blissfully ignorant of the troubles in store for us, and slept that healthy, sound sleep, which only those who pass their lives among the pure air of lake and mountain can ever hope to enjoy.

* * * * *

Crash——!

I awoke and found the yacht trembling. My first impression was that a boat had blundered into us; my second, that we were being boarded by a gang of moonlighters who had come to steal my guns. I jumped out of my bunk, and with a little six-shooter in my hand went on deck. No boat was to be seen. The lake, from which the darkness was just lifting, was calm as I had left it the previous evening, and a dull red glow in the eastward showed that dawn was at hand. It was very strange.

Our man, who had also been awakened, was looking out of the hatchway, but could give no explanation of the strange noise, so I turned in again, mightily puzzled, and was just falling off to sleep when there came another crash, greater than the first, and the yacht shook with the blow. Again I went on deck, but again learned nothing; for there was the lake, quiet as before, and no boat in sight.

"Could it have been the wind, sorr?" whispered my man, who was pale, and looked frightened. He had just spoken when the storm answered the question. A great blast suddenly struck the yacht, blurring the smooth surface of the lake and nearly carrying me off my feet. It died away instantly. I waited a few minutes on deck, and very shortly received another staggering blow from the coming tempest. This gust was followed by others, the period between them each time decreasing, until in about half an hour or less there was one long, angry roar, and the yacht was straining at her anchor-chain. The lake which had been seething, gradually rose, and a heavy swell poured in through the narrow mouth of the bay. I had fondly imagined no danger could have come to us through such a narrow portal, and was amazed to find that we were moored in a terribly exposed position.

Fiercer and louder roared the wind; the yacht rolled and pitched; the crockery which the man had left unwashed from the night's supper, tumbled on the floor of the cuddy, and was broken to smithereens. Everything on the deck was swept from it, including a large hamper full of bottles—soda-water, beer, and wine. A seven-foot Berthon boat, the *Mouse's* punt, which we had hauled on deck the previous evening, was being lifted up when I caught her, and though nearly taken overboard myself, just saved her in time, and lashed her down firmly.

We had riding astern of us two fishing boats. The painter of one of these was weak, and at the commencement of the gale broke, and the boat was swept ashore. After this, from time to time, I looked very carefully after the other, and felt confident that it was safe. But the constant plunging of both the boat and the yacht caused the stout, new painter of the former to chafe, and to our dismay, shortly after I had made fast the Berthon, we saw our only means of reaching land drift away from us. I thought the cot would have been smashed up on the rocks, but she just escaped a rugged point and went on to the sand. The instant her keel touched the bottom the wind lifted her up and rolled her over and over like an air-ball, carrying her quite thirty yards up the shore from the water's edge. And this, mind, was a heavy lake boat some eighteen feet in length.

To reach the shore in the little Berthon boat was an impossibility, so now we gave all our attention to saving the yacht, for our two big anchors were dragging. We paid out every inch of chain we could spare, but still, with every uplifting of the bows of the yacht, there came such a terrific tug on the anchors that they moved a foot or more. Had the wind been in any other direction we should have been safe enough, but blowing down the Killaloe reach and straight across the lake into the mouth of the little bay we were in almost as heavy a sea as if we had been outside.

And now to my great grief the *Mouse* which was moored near a reed bed and between us and the pine wood began to drag her anchor. In a very few minutes she went aground a solitary rock which projected from the sand, knocking a considerable hole in her bottom. She fortunately lay where the swell hardly affected her, for the violence of the wind forced her right through a reed bed and into very shoal water. That she dragged her anchor, which was of a sufficient size for ordinary purposes, after her through the reeds, will give some idea of the fury of the gale.

Still the wind increased, and now the air became full of water. All of us were drenched to the skin. I could hear the voices of people shouting on the shore some fifty yards away, but could only see them dimly through the spindrift. Under our stern was a small reef of limestone rocks on which it seemed fated, if the gale held, we should be driven, for with every big roller that entered the bay the yacht was lifted up and carried a few inches nearer to destruction.

I racked my brain in vain to think of some means of holding her, something to weight the chain and keep it on the bottom. Owing to the force of the wind the chain was being strained tight, and instead of several fathoms of it lying on the bottom and causing the pull on the anchor to be in a horizontal direction, the pull was upwards, and every uplifting of the yacht's bows on a wave caused a displacement of the anchors.

Finally I bethought me of the yacht's stove. If this could be run down the chain by any means, the weight might be sufficient to keep the last few fathoms of chain on the bottom, in which case the anchors would, I thought, hold fast. It was a heavy little stove, but we soon unshipped it and carried it on deck. Then our troubles began. The gale was now so furious that to stand upright was impossible, and the decks were running with water. We had to crawl on hands and knees, pushing the stove in front of us, until we got to the bows, and there held on. The noise of the wind was deafening, and neither could hear the other speak. I passed a short piece of stout rope through the front of the grate and out at the top, clasping the two ends round the cable and fastening them together. Then we heaved the stove overboard and sent this extraordinary messenger down to the anchors. I feared it would stick on the journey, but the tugging of the yacht on her cable jerked it down the chain, and very soon it disappeared beneath the water. How anxiously we watched our marks on the shore, to see if the yacht was moving! Great indeed was our joy when we found that the stove had turned the scale, for we no longer drifted towards the ugly group of rocks which frowned at us from the shore.

There was now quite a crowd of watchers anxiously awaiting the disaster which seemed imminent, but the stove, coupled with a certain amount of good fortune, saved us, for about 7 o'clock the wind suddenly chopped round to the westward, and though it blew harder than ever, the pine-wood sheltered us, the swell at our end of the lough subsided, and the yacht was safe. The crowd now turned their attention to our fishing boat, which they righted, carried down to the shore, and launched. After some consultation two local fishermen and two members of the constabulary got into the little craft and rowed out to us, giving us to understand that they were to be considered heroes for having saved us at the risk of their lives. But at the time I would not have minded going ashore myself in the little seven-foot Berthon.

And so the stove saved the yacht, but it was a martyr in the cause, for when we got under way a few days later we found only a few bits of old iron clinging on to the chain; all the rest of the stove had been smashed up against the anchors. How roofs were taken off, hay-stacks blown to pieces, and great trees which had stood the tempests of a hundred years were levelled to ground, I need not tell. Suffice it to say it was a magnificent, all-powerful storm, the like of which I never expect, nor indeed wish, to see again.

* * * * *

And now the end, and it is an ending to which I come reluctantly, for in the writing and revision of these reminiscences of the Sister Isle, memories the most pleasant have been revived, kindly faces have gathered round me, the sound of the rich Tipperary brogue has sounded sweetly in my ears. Trout have risen again to my drifting Mayfly, large pike have savagely rushed at spinning bait, snipe have twisted and turned to evade those deadly pellets. How the amber-coloured waves curled on the rock-bound lake, and the clouds gathered round the summits of the Killaloe mountains, the good yacht heeling over to the squalls which come tearing down the gorges. Quack! quack! and three fat wild ducks depart in haste with much ado from the reed-bed in Youghal Bay, and a flock of curlew with shrill pipings rise from the shores. Or are we on the moorlands in Charles O'Malley's country, near Meelick of hospitable memories and those shots are accounting for grouse after grouse? Then the Winter—the ringing of the skates, the long sails after wildfowl, the flight shooting, the encounter with the savage cattle on Holy

Island; and the Spring at fair Mountshannon, with its shoals of sturdy gillaroos.

Wild Coos Bay, too, where great perch haunt the weed-beds and the wildfowl swim undisturbed. Or are we now ascending to the rolling moorlands of Clare, gazing out over that fair, wide expanse of island-studded water on to the mountains of Kerry far distant, presently, after mooring our tent on the sloping shore, to be whipping the rippling waters of Lough Creina, Harry in the bows of the old dinghy and trout swimming about our bare ankles in water which we have no time to bale, so fast do the fish rise.—Dear Shannon friends and scenes, I love you all. To you and the reader, Greeting and Farewell.

"Thus shall memory often in dreams sublime
   Catch a glimpse of the days that are over;
Thus, sighing, look through the waves of Time
   For the long-faded glories they cover."

THE END.

HARDY'S "GOLD MEDAL" RODS
AND TACKLE ARE BEYOND COMPETITION.

THE BEST SALMON AND TROUT RODS MADE ARE
The "**KELSON**," £12 5s. (18ft. Cane-Built Steel Centre); The "**HI-REGAN**," £10 (16ft. Cane-Built Steel Centre); The "**CHOLMONDELEY-PENNELL**," £9 5s. (14ft. Cane-Built Steel Centre); The "**SPECIALS**," £5 16s. 6d. each (11ft. and 12ft. Cane-Built Steel Centre).

The "**ALNWICK**" Greenheart Rods are superior to all other Makers' Wood Rods.

IMPORTANT.—If you want the best of everything in Rods, Flies, Tackle, &c., write us, it will pay you. Remember the "Best" is always the Cheapest.

Highest Awards in the World. 35 Medals.

CATALOGUE over Three Hundred Illustration 260 Pages, FREE!

The "FIELD" says:—"It ought never to be forgotten that it is to Messrs. of Alnwick, we owe the supremacy we have achieved as rod makers."

Mr. J. J. Hardy, the "Champion of the World," making his Record Cast of 39yds. 1ft. 9in. with an 18ft. Steel Centre Rod.

HARDY. BROS., ALNWICK, Eng.

BRANCHES :
- 61, PALL MALL, LONDON.
- 5, SOUTH ST. DAVID STREET, EDINBURGH.
- 12 & 14, MOULT STREET, MANCHESTER.

INDEX.

"Get a thorough insight into the index by which the whole book is governed and turned, like fishes, by the tail."—SWIFT.

INDEX.

Andy, Deserted by, 176
Angling, Philosophy of, 111
Angling, Uncertainty of, 112
Athlone Eel Boys, 178
Athlone, Pike Fishing at, in Winter, 6

Baits Preserved in Spirits, 17
Ballyracket Hall, Christmas at, 198
Battering-ram, The, 25
Bishop of Killaloe, and the Pike, 206
Blue Heads, 179
Bog, A run over the, 76
Boycot, A, 27
Brady, Pat, 25
Brian Boru, Legend of, 85
Brian Boru's Castle, 84
Bryan Borovy, 81

Cabin, an Irish, 72
Calm, Caught in a, 116
Camping Out, 59
Carrigeen Islands, 50
Castles of Irish Chieftains, 88

Char, Irish, 55
Chub-fly for Trout, 77
Clonmacnoise, 8
Clonoolia Bay, 44
Clonoolia Bay, Furious storm in, 219
Cooz Bay, 184
Coot or Duck, 123
Coots, Boiled, 7-10
Coot, Strange Legend of a, 6
Cribby Island, 50
Cross, Ancient Irish, 9
Crossed lines, Disadvantages of, 43
Cross on the door, The, 75
Cuilceath, 159
Curlew Killed by Frost, 124

Damming the Breeding Stream, 78-80
Dapping, 104
Dapping, Tackle for, 46
Dapping, The art of, 49
Disillusioned, 10
Doctor, The, and the Rudd, 191
Dolochan, 139
Dromineer Bay, Skating in, 128

Dromineer Bay, Yacht Racing in, 174
Dromineer May-fly Fishing, 45
Duck Shooting from Yacht, 14

Eel Catching as an Industry, 178
Eels, Bait for, 178
Eviction, Story of, 86

Fairy Tale of Lough Derg, 51
Fisherman's Luck, 113
Flies, Shower of, 117
Flight-shooting, 94
Fly-fishing for Rudd, 192
Fog, Lost in the, 125
Fog, Wildfowling in, 121-125

Gandola, A, 55
Geese, Wild, Stalking, 166
Gillaroo as food, 103
Gillaroo cutlets, 52
Gillaroo, Food of, 107
Gillaroo, Is it a species? 105-108
Golden plover, A shot at, 160
Gort-glas, 56
Grilse, An unexpected, 115

Heather Burning, 70
Hedge, An Irish, 144
Holy Island, 157
Holy Island in Winter, 166
Holy Island, Legend of, 158
Hooker, A leaky, 55
House Building in Ireland, 140

Ice, Breaking out of the, 163
Ilanmore, 50
Ireland, Condition of, 23
Irish Costume, 75

Killaloe, Accomodation at, 46
Killaloe, May-fly Fishing at, 45
Killaloe, Snipe-shooting at, 84-96
Killaloe, Storms at, 212
Kilrush River, The, 26

Lake Perch-fishing, 182-186
Lake, The Frozen, 129
Land-league Hunt, 44
Land-league Machine, The, 30
Loch Leven Trout in Captivi 106
Lost on the Lake, 168
Lough Creina, 67
Lough Derg, Storms on, 212-227
Lough Rea, 4
Lough Trout Fishing, 68

Married in Camera, 65
May-flies eaten by Eels, 47
May-fly Fishing, 45-104
May-fly Fishing, Tackle for, 46
May-fly, Rise of on Lough Derg, 45
May-fly Season on Lough Derg, 43
Meelick, Wildfowling at, 13
Miltown Malbay, 74-75
Moonlighters, 29
Mount Shannon, 44, 214
Mount Shannon, May-fly Fishing at, 45
Mouse, Alone on the, 176
Mouse, The, 174
Mouse, The, in a Storm, 218
Murder, Attempted, 31

INDEX. 233

Narcissus, Wild, 158

Otter Snaring Attempted, 31
Overboard, 175

Padneen Honan, 61
Paternostering in Coos Bay, 185
Perch, Baits for, 181
Perch Fry Catching, 177-180
Perch, How to cook, 181
Phantoms, Silver, 100
Phantom, Red, 15
Photograph, A spoilt, 62
Pike, A twenty-five pounder, 18
Pike, big Irish, 3
Pike-fishing in Winter, 157
Pike-fishing round the Weeds, 100
Pike-fishing, Winter, on Shannon, 14
Pike, In pursuit of, 202-208
Pike Legends, 197
Pike, The forty pound, 197
Pike, Twenty-five Pounder, 19
Pike, Weighting the, 206
Pochards, Sailing down on, 165
Police Huts, 31
Preserved Baits, 100

Rats, Boarded by, 35
Rat-catching, 36-39
Red Phantom as Pike Bait, 15
Rinskaheen, 127
Roach Distinguished from Rudd, 190
Roach in Ireland, 189
Round Tower, 11
Round Towers, 158
Rudd, Description of, 190

Rudd Distinguished from Roach, 190
Rudd Fishing, 189-194
Rudd on the Shallows, 125

Salmo Estuarius, 136
Salmon, A lost, 100
Salmon Fishing in Lough Derg, 127
Salmon, Scarcity of, in Lough Derg, 128
Salmo Orcadensis, 136
Salmo Stomachicus, 104
Scariff Bay, 18
Scariff Bay, Frozen in, 160
Sergeant, The mysterious, 60
Seven Churches, Ruins of, 8
Shannon, Better preservation wanted, 128
Shannon Estuary, The, 55
Shebeen, In a, 201
Short rising fish, 149
Shrew Mouse eaten by Trout, 149
Signalling with box matches, 169
Sinbad, 12
Skating on the Lake, 124
Slieve Callan, 67
Slob-trout, 135-151
Slob-trout Fishing, 140
Slob-trout, Origin of, 136
Slob-trout, where found, 139
Snipe, Extraordinary Numbers of, 91
Snipe-shooting, 83-96
Spawning, Early, 153
Storm on the Mountains, 76

Taxidermist, Williams of Dublin, 19

Tim Delaney's Bull, 166
Trout, A. for Dinner, 114
Trout, Colour of, 69
Trout, Curious Spawning Habits of, 67
Trout Monster, Exhibition of, 117
Trout, Relations of, 106
Trout Rising by thousands, 74
Trout, Spawning habits of, 77
Trout, Variations of, 106

Wild Duck Shooting, 95
Wild Fowling at Meelick, 13
Wild Fowl Preserve, A, 15

Yacht Racing on Lough Derg, 173
Yacht Stove, saved by the, 224

www.ingramcontent.com/pod-product-compliance
Lightning Source LLC
Chambersburg PA
CBHW031740230426
43669CB00007B/419